Don Webster

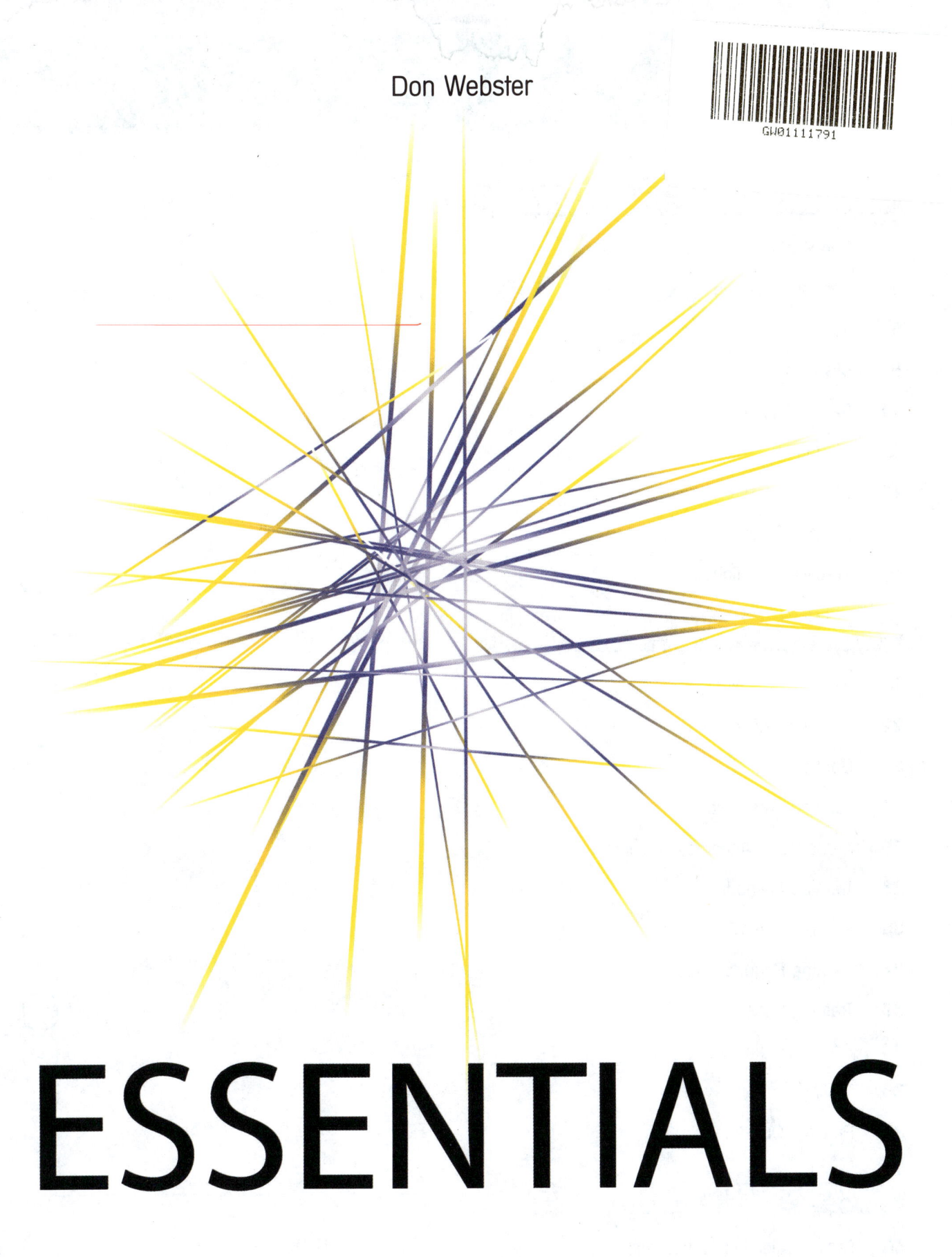

ESSENTIALS

GCSE Physical Education
Revision Guide

Contents

Body Systems
Revised

- 4 The Skeleton
- 5 Vertebral Column
- 6 Joints
- 8 Muscles
- 10 Respiratory System
- 12 Circulatory System
- 14 Blood Pressure
- 15 Effects of Exercise
- 16 Practice Questions

Fitness and Training

- 18 Reasons for Exercise
- 22 Principles of Training
- 23 Goal Setting
- 24 Training Threshold
- 25 Aerobic and Anaerobic Training
- 26 Training Methods
- 30 Programmes of Exercise
- 31 Training Requirements
- 32 Training Sessions
- 33 Effects of Exercise
- 35 Testing
- 38 Practice Questions

Factors Affecting Performance

- 40 Factors Affecting Performance
- 44 Skill
- 46 Drugs in Sport
- 48 Practice Questions

Contents

Participation in Sport

Revised

- 50 Taking Part ☐
- 52 Participation ☐
- 54 The Way to Play ☐
- 56 Modern Technology ☐
- 58 Training Aids ☐
- 59 Playing Safe ☐
- 61 Lifting and Carrying ☐
- 62 Practice Questions ☐

Issues in Sport

- 64 Sponsorship ☐
- 66 Media ☐
- 68 Politics ☐
- 70 Sporting Behaviour ☐
- 72 Sporting Status ☐
- 74 Discrimination ☐
- 78 Practice Questions ☐

Organisation in Sport

- 80 Sport in School ☐
- 81 Facilities ☐
- 82 Organisation of Sport ☐
- 84 Promoting Excellence ☐
- 86 Promoting International Sport ☐
- 87 Funding for Sport ☐
- 88 Practice Questions ☐

- 90 Appendix
- 91 Glossary
- 93 Answers
- 96 Index

The Skeleton

The Skeleton and its Functions

The **skeleton** has **four functions**:
- The **protection** of soft parts, such as the **brain** and the **lungs**.
- **Blood formation** – this happens in the **marrow** of the long bones.
- **Movement** – you can't walk or bend without bones.
- **Support** – the skeleton gives you **shape** and holds vital organs in place.

There are **206 bones in the body** and they fall into four types:
- **Long bones**, e.g. femur.
- **Short bones**, e.g. phalanges.
- **Flat bones**, e.g. scapula.
- **Irregular bones**, e.g. vertebrae.

The skeleton is divided into two main parts:
- The **appendicular** skeleton contains the moving parts that are **not connected** to the vertebral column. These have a large amount of movement.
- The **axial** skeleton consists of the **vertebral column** and the bones **connected to it**. These have only a small amount of movement.

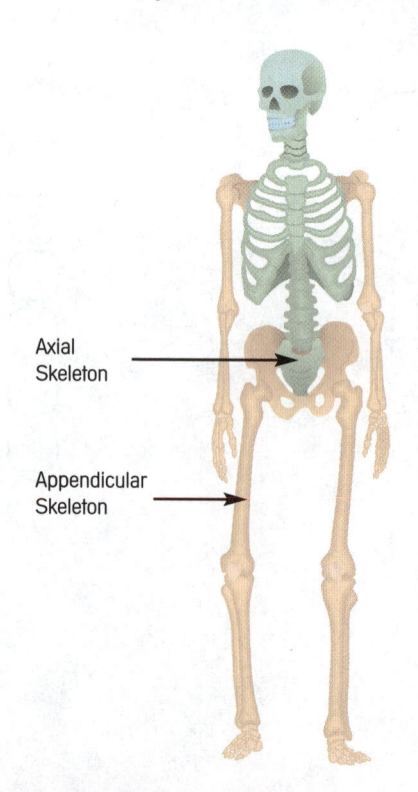

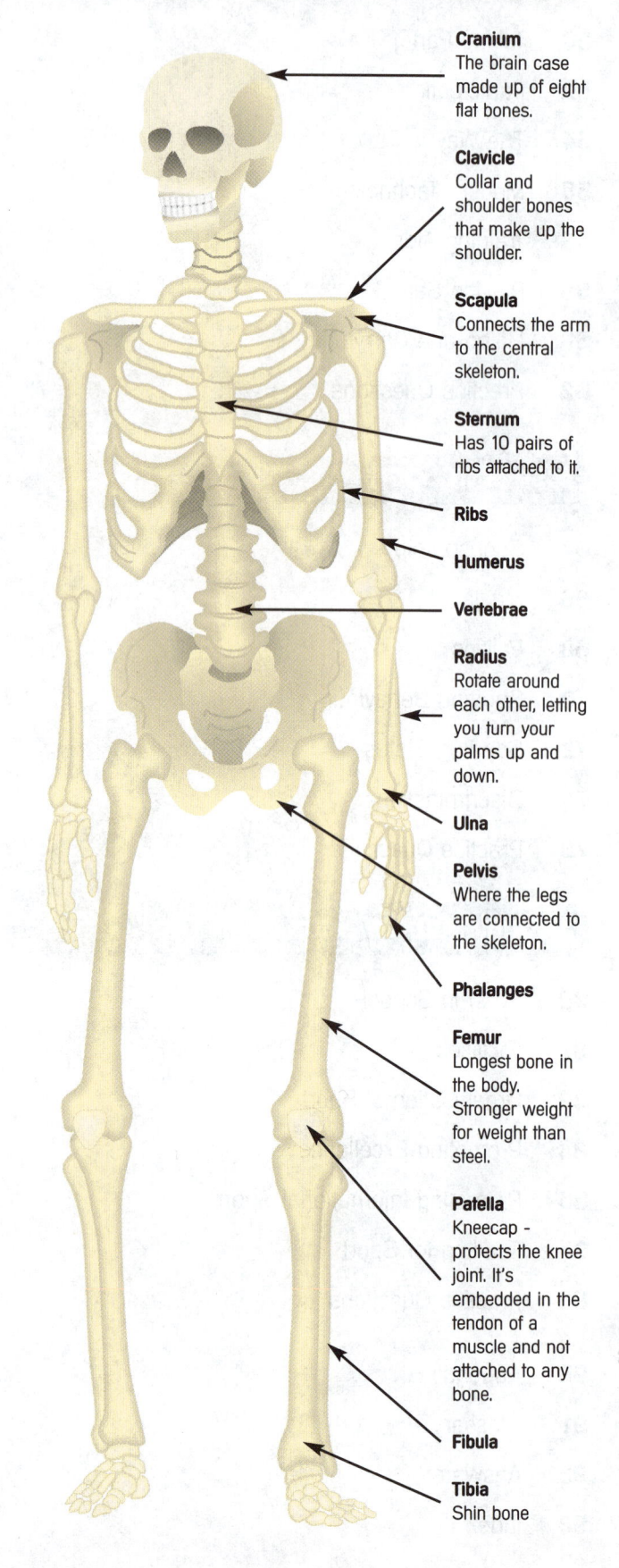

Axial Skeleton

Appendicular Skeleton

Cranium
The brain case made up of eight flat bones.

Clavicle
Collar and shoulder bones that make up the shoulder.

Scapula
Connects the arm to the central skeleton.

Sternum
Has 10 pairs of ribs attached to it.

Ribs

Humerus

Vertebrae

Radius
Rotate around each other, letting you turn your palms up and down.

Ulna

Pelvis
Where the legs are connected to the skeleton.

Phalanges

Femur
Longest bone in the body. Stronger weight for weight than steel.

Patella
Kneecap - protects the knee joint. It's embedded in the tendon of a muscle and not attached to any bone.

Fibula

Tibia
Shin bone

Vertebral Column

Vertebrae

The **vertebral column** (backbone) is made up of **29 vertebrae**. These are all separate bones except for those that make up the **coccyx**. These four are **fused together**.

The joints between each pair of vertebrae…
- only move a little
- don't have a great range of individual movement
- can all move in **any direction** when they're all working together.

The two vertebrae at the top of the column are called the **atlas** and **axis** vertebrae. The atlas sits on a pin that sticks up from the axis. This allows the head to move in all directions, from nodding to turning.

Between each pair of vertebrae that move is a small disc of **cartilage** that **allows the bones to move without friction**.

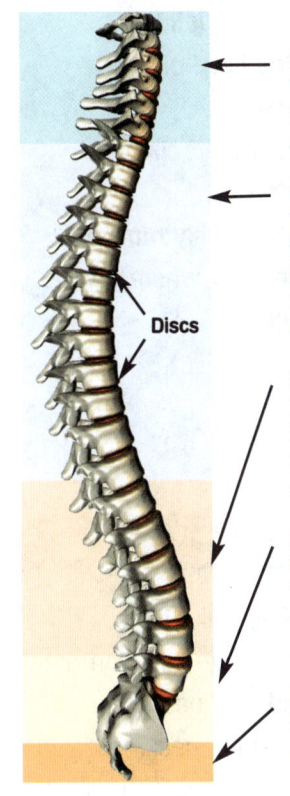

7 Cervical Vertebrae
These neck vertebrae allow your head to bend, tilt and nod. The first two (atlas and axis) allow head rotation.

12 Thoracic Vertebrae
These have projections for attachment of the ribs. Flexion and extension can occur and a small degree of rotation, but movement is limited compared to the cervical vertebrae.

Discs

5 Lumbar Vertebrae
These are in the waist region. They're large and provide attachment for the back muscles as they endure the most stress in walking and support.

5 Sacral Vertebrae
These are fused to form one piece. Together with the pelvis they form the pelvic (hip) girdle to which the legs are attached.

4 Coccyx
These are fused together and form the remnants of what was a tail in our evolutionary past.

Functions of the Column

The **functions** of the column are…
- **support** – the column or backbone transfers the weight down to the **pelvis**
- **movement** – the column as a whole allows movement in **all directions**
- **protection** – inside the vertebrae are bundles of nerves that make up the **spinal cord**, which helps control all body functions.

Quick Test

1. How many bones are there in the body?
2. Where is blood formed?
3. Which bones make up the axial skeleton?
4. What is attached to the thoracic vertebrae?
5. Where are the atlas and axis bones found?

KEY WORDS
Make sure you understand these words before moving on!
- Protection
- Blood formation
- Movement
- Support
- Long bone
- Short bone
- Flat bone
- Irregular bone
- Appendicular
- Axial
- Atlas
- Axis
- Cartilage

Joints

Types of Joint

The following are the main types of **joint**:
- **Fibrous** – sometimes called **fixed** or **immovable**; found in the **skull**.
- **Cartilaginous** – sometimes called **slightly movable**; found in the **vertebrae**.
- **Synovial** – sometimes called **freely movable**; found in **most parts of the body** where a wide range of movement happens.

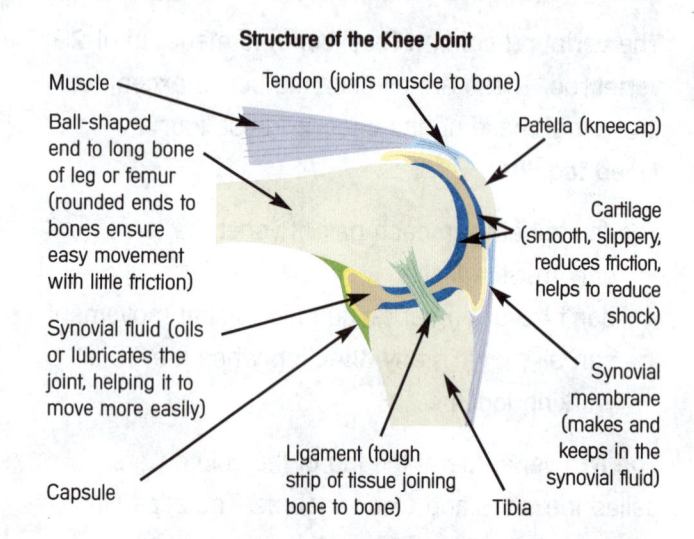

Structure of the Knee Joint
- Muscle
- Ball-shaped end to long bone of leg or femur (rounded ends to bones ensure easy movement with little friction)
- Synovial fluid (oils or lubricates the joint, helping it to move more easily)
- Capsule
- Tendon (joins muscle to bone)
- Patella (kneecap)
- Cartilage (smooth, slippery, reduces friction, helps to reduce shock)
- Synovial membrane (makes and keeps in the synovial fluid)
- Ligament (tough strip of tissue joining bone to bone)
- Tibia

Synovial Joints

The following are the types of **synovial joint**:
- **Hinge** – allows movement in one direction only, for example, the elbow and the knee.
- **Pivot** – allows for **rotation** at the neck.
- **Ball and socket** – allows for as full a range of movement as possible, for example, the hip.
- **Saddle** – allows movement in **two** directions, for example, base of thumb joint.
- **Condyloid** – allows movement **forwards**, **backwards** and **sideways**, but **not** rotation, for example, the wrist.

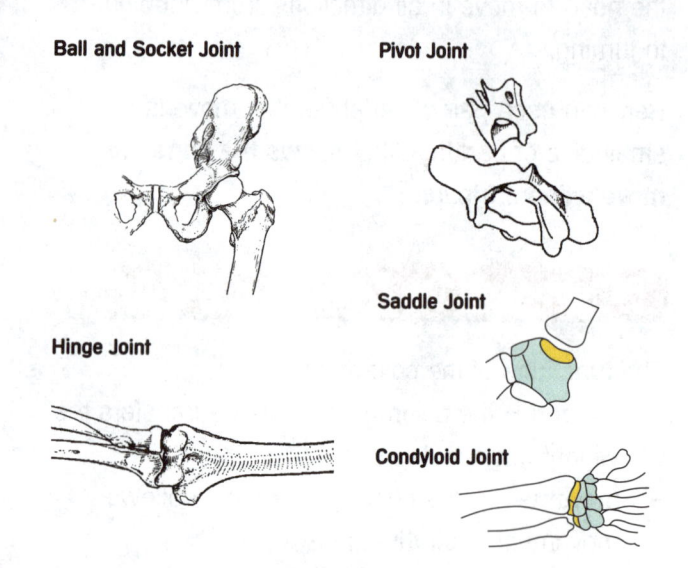

Ball and Socket Joint

Hinge Joint

Pivot Joint

Saddle Joint

Condyloid Joint

Joints

Joints are protected and connected by...
- **articular cartilage** – found at the ends of long bones; very hard and **protects** the ends of the bone
- **meniscal cartilage** (menisci plural, meniscus singular) – found between the ends of long bones; acts as **shock absorber**
- **ligaments** – these hold bones **together** and are strong and non-elastic, but **flexible**
- **synovial fluid** – found between the bones; it's held in a **membrane** and **lubricates** the bones as they move.

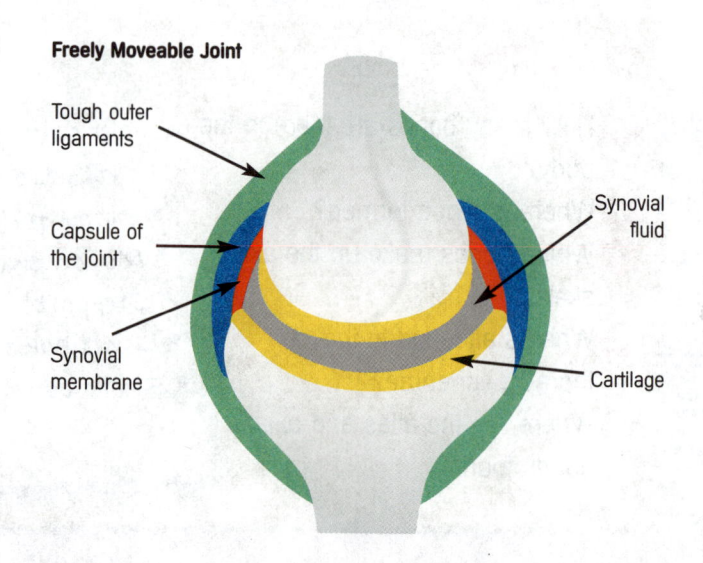

Freely Moveable Joint
- Tough outer ligaments
- Capsule of the joint
- Synovial membrane
- Synovial fluid
- Cartilage

Joints

Types of Joint Movement

There are several types of joint movement:
- **Flexion** – when a joint **closes**.
- **Extension** – when a joint **opens**.
- **Abduction** – when a body part moves **away** from the centre of the body.
- **Adduction** – when a body part moves **towards** the centre of the body.
- **Circumduction** – when the end of a bone **draws a circle** as it moves.
- **Rotation** – when a bone moves **round a pivot point**.

Joints and Movement

This table shows the joints that can perform movements.

	Hinge	Ball and Socket	Pivot	Condyloid	Saddle	Gliding
Flexion	✓	✓		✓	✓	A small amount of these types of movement
Extension	✓	✓		✓	✓	
Abduction		✓		✓	✓	
Adduction		✓		✓	✓	
Rotation		✓	✓			
Circumduction		✓				

Joints and Muscles

Joints and muscles work together because…
- bones can't move on their own
- movement is caused by **muscle contraction**
- muscles are attached to bones by **tendons**
- bones are attached to each other by **ligaments**.

Overuse at Joints

Joints can suffer certain conditions from repeated use:
- **Inflammation** – redness, heat, swelling, pain.
- **Arthritis** – conditions that result in inflammation of the joint.
- **Osteoarthritis** – specific form of arthritis caused by articular cartilage wearing away.
- **Lupus** – autoimmune condition causing inflammation at the joints.

Sufferers should **avoid repeated impact** on affected joints, e.g. jumping on hard surfaces. Activities that place **less stress** on the joints are best e.g. cycling, swimming.

KEY WORDS
Make sure you understand these words before moving on!
- Fibrous
- Synovial
- Cartilage
- Ligament
- Flexion
- Extension
- Tendon

Muscles

Types of Muscles

There are three types of muscles:
- **Involuntary** or **smooth** – found in the walls of **blood vessels** and the **gut**. These stretch as needed but work automatically.
- **Voluntary** or skeletal – attached to the skeleton and help to make the body's **shape**. They cause movement but have to be **told to work**.
- **Cardiac** – only found in the heart. Its only job is to **pump blood** round the body. It adjusts its speed as needed and works **automatically** at all times.

Where Voluntary Muscles Perform

Deltoids create abduction at the shoulder and raise your arm sideways, e.g. swimming arm action.

Pectorals create adduction at the shoulder across the chest, e.g. press-ups.

Biceps cause flexion at the elbow, e.g. chin-ups.

Abdominals allow you to flex your trunk, e.g. sit-ups.

Quadriceps make extension of the leg possible at the knee, e.g. squats, kicking.

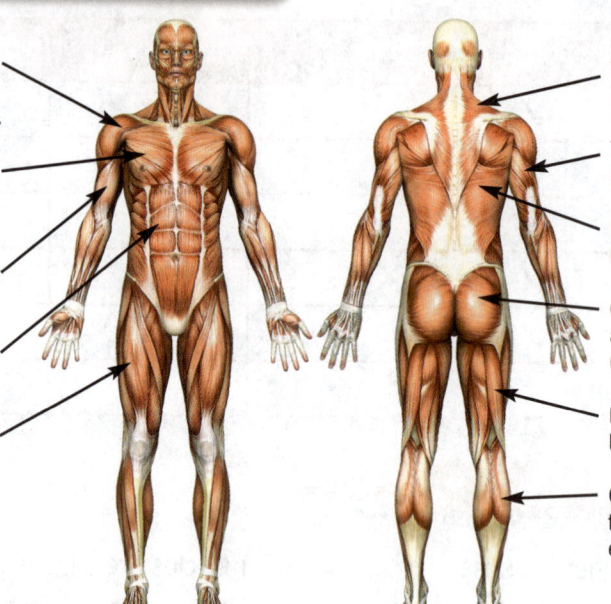

Trapezius allows rotation of the shoulders, e.g. cricket bowling action.

Triceps create extension at the elbow, e.g. press-ups, throwing.

Latissimus allows adduction at the shoulder behind your back, e.g. rope climb.

Gluteals allow extension, abduction and adduction at the hip, e.g. squats, jumping. (Gluteus Maximus is the biggest Gluteal).

Hamstrings allow flexion of the leg at the knee, e.g. sprinting (leg action recovery).

Gastrocnemius allows you to stand on tiptoes, by creating extension at the ankle, e.g. sprinting (start).

How Muscles Work

Muscles work by **contraction** and **relaxation**. Voluntary muscles are attached to bones by **tendons**.

Muscles work mainly in pairs – whilst one pulls or contracts (**gets shorter**), the other relaxes (**gets longer**). This is called **working antagonistically**.

The **agonist** or **prime mover** is the muscle doing the work. It contracts to pull on the bone. The **antagonist** is the muscle that relaxes to let the movement take effect. **Synergists** are muscles that assist in the action of the prime mover. They **stabilise the joint**, preventing undesirable movement.

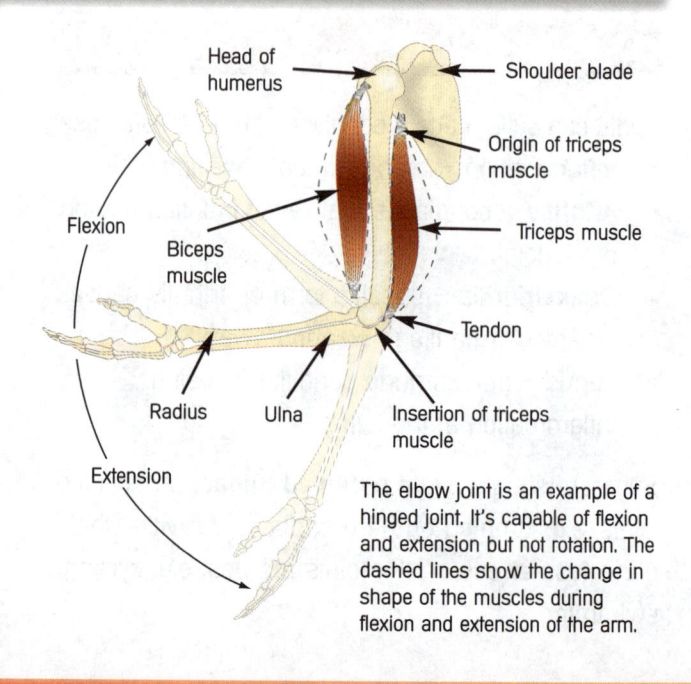

The elbow joint is an example of a hinged joint. It's capable of flexion and extension but not rotation. The dashed lines show the change in shape of the muscles during flexion and extension of the arm.

Muscles

Types of Fibre

Voluntary muscles consist of **two types of fibre**, but their proportions vary in different people:

- **Fast twitch fibres** are **powerful**, and they **work quickly** and **explosively**. They're good for sprinting and speed events, but **get tired very quickly**.
- **Slow twitch fibres** work in a **slow, steady, sustained** manner. These are good for endurance events such as the marathon. They **get tired less quickly**.

Fast Twitch	Slow Twitch
Shorter	Longer
Thicker	Thinner
Contract quickly	Contract slowly
Exhaust quickly	Exhaust slowly

Types of Contraction

- **Isometric contractions** – the muscle fibres **stay the same length** and the bones **don't move**. This type of contraction takes place in a scrum or when you push your hands together.
- **Isotonic contractions** – the muscle fibres **change length** and the bones **move**.
- **Concentric contractions** – the muscle fibres get **shorter**.
- **Eccentric contractions** – the muscle fibres **lengthen under tension**.

An example of muscle contraction is the arm curl: the biceps **contract concentrically** whilst the triceps **lengthen eccentrically**.

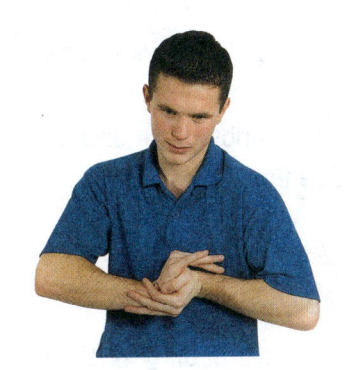

Isometric Contraction

Isotonic Contraction

Quick Test

1. Where in the body are…
   a) the deltoids?   b) the gastrocnemius?
   c) the gluteals?
2. Where is smooth muscle found?
3. What is the other name for a prime mover?
4. What type of muscle fibres are best for sprinters?
5. What happens to muscle fibres during isometric contractions?

KEY WORDS
Make sure you understand these words before moving on!
- Involuntary
- Smooth
- Voluntary
- Cardiac
- Agonist
- Antagonist
- Synergist
- Isometric contraction
- Isotonic contraction
- Concentric contraction
- Eccentric contraction

Respiratory System

Breathing

The main body parts used in breathing are the...
- **nasal passages**
- **windpipe** (trachea)
- **lungs**.

The lungs are found within the **thoracic cavity** (chest), protected by the ribs and the **diaphragm**.

To breathe in (**inspiration**), these actions increase the size of the thoracic cavity and **air is sucked in**:
- **Intercostal muscles** pull the ribs **forward and upwards**.
- The diaphragm is **pulled down**.

To breathe out (**expiration**), these actions **squeeze the air out**:
- **Intercostal muscles** pull the ribs **down and in**.
- The diaphragm is **pulled up**.

Standard Respiratory System — Nasal passages, Ribs, Lungs, Alveoli, Trachea, Thorax (chest), Intercostal muscles, Diaphragm

Inspiration: Ribs are raised; Diaphragm flattens as diaphragm muscle contracts.

Expiration: Rib cage lowered; Diaphragm raised.

Gaseous Exchange

Gaseous exchange is the transfer of **oxygen** (O_2) and **carbon dioxide** (CO_2) between the lungs and the capillaries that surround the alveoli:

1. Oxygen from the air is passed through the thin walls of the alveoli to the red cells in the blood. This process is called **oxygen uptake**.
2. Carbon dioxide is passed from the blood through the thin walls of the **capillaries** into the **alveolus**.

Into the Lungs	Out of the Lungs
Oxygen (21%)	Oxygen is reduced because your body has used some
Carbon dioxide (tiny amount)	Carbon dioxide is increased because your body produces it
Water vapour (a little)	Water increases as a by-product of aerobic respiration
Nitrogen (79%)	Nitrogen is a component of air that your body doesn't use or produce, so the amount stays the same

A Single Alveolus and a Capillary

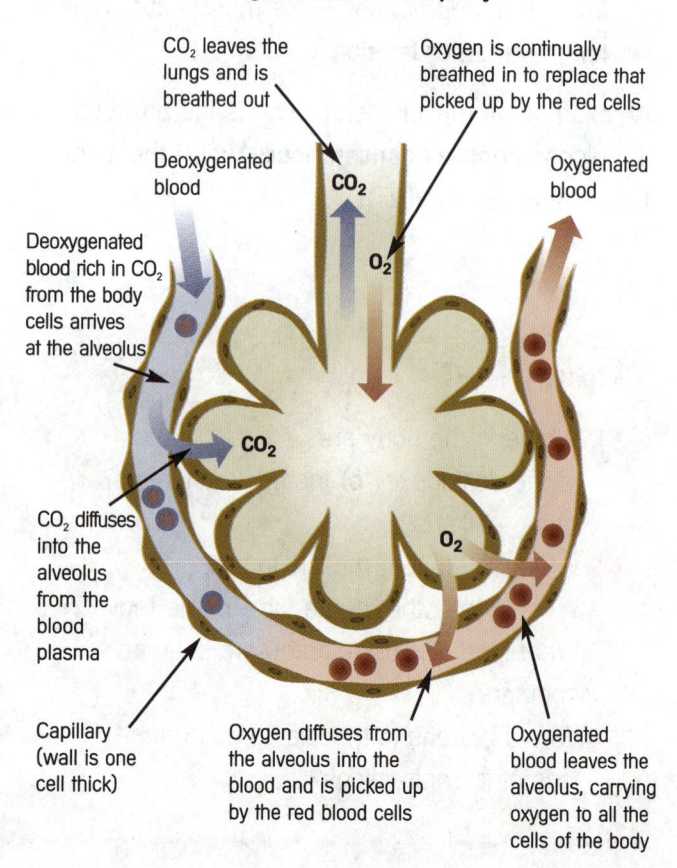

- CO_2 leaves the lungs and is breathed out
- Oxygen is continually breathed in to replace that picked up by the red cells
- Deoxygenated blood
- Oxygenated blood
- Deoxygenated blood rich in CO_2 from the body cells arrives at the alveolus
- CO_2 diffuses into the alveolus from the blood plasma
- Capillary (wall is one cell thick)
- Oxygen diffuses from the alveolus into the blood and is picked up by the red blood cells
- Oxygenated blood leaves the alveolus, carrying oxygen to all the cells of the body

Respiratory System

Gaseous Exchange (cont.)

Gaseous exchange depends on…
- **vital capacity** – the maximum amount of air you can breath in and out
- **VO_2** – the amount of oxygen you can absorb in one minute
- **tidal volume** – the amount of air you breathe in and out in **one breath**
- **respiratory rate** – how many breaths you can take in one minute
- **minute volume** – the total volume of air breathed in and out in one minute.

Tidal Volume x Respiratory Rate = Minute Volume

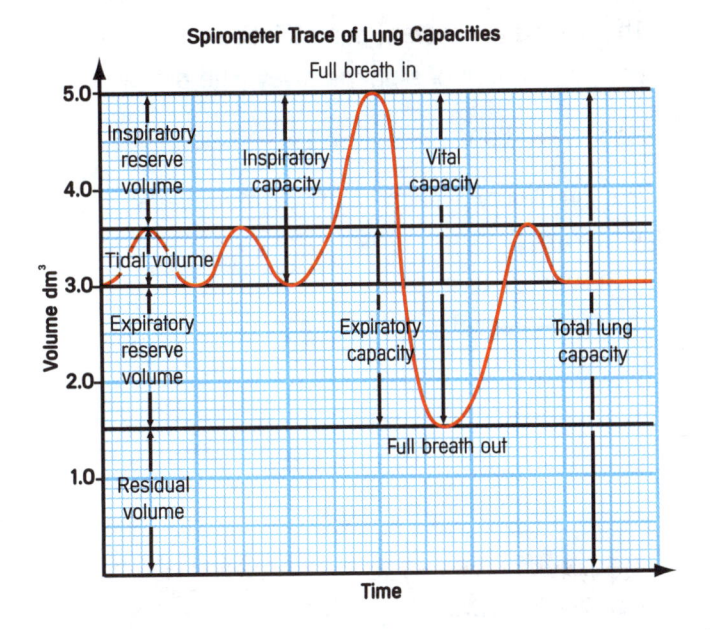

Spirometer Trace of Lung Capacities

(Graph showing Full breath in, Inspiratory reserve volume, Inspiratory capacity, Vital capacity, Tidal volume, Expiratory reserve volume, Expiratory capacity, Total lung capacity, Full breath out, Residual volume; y-axis Volume dm³ from 1.0 to 5.0; x-axis Time)

Response to Exercise

The type of exercise affects the gaseous exchange.

Aerobic exercise…
- is **low intensity** activity
- uses **O_2** to produce energy
- produces **waste by-products** CO_2 and H_2O (water)
- can be carried out for **long periods of time**
- needs a **shorter recovery time**.

Glucose + Oxygen = Energy + H_2O + CO_2

Anaerobic exercise…
- is **high intensity** activity
- uses **glucose** rather than O_2 to produce energy
- produces the **poisonous waste by-product lactic acid**
- is caused by lack of oxygen (**oxygen debt**)
- can only be carried out for a **short time**
- needs a **longer recovery time**.

Glucose → Small amount of Energy + Lactic Acid

Quick Test
1. Where are the intercostal muscles?
2. What does expiration mean?
3. Where are the alveoli?
4. What is the respiratory rate?
5. What kind of activity is aerobic exercise?

KEY WORDS
Make sure you understand these words before moving on!
- Inspiration
- Expiration
- Vital capacity
- VO_2
- Tidal volume
- Minute volume
- Aerobic exercise
- Anaerobic exercise
- Lactic acid
- Oxygen debt

Circulatory System

Circulatory System

The **circulatory system** pumps blood round the body in a **figure of eight pathway**. The pathway is:

Heart → Lungs → Heart → Body → Heart

The circulatory system has three main parts:
- **Heart**
- **Blood**
- **Blood vessels**.

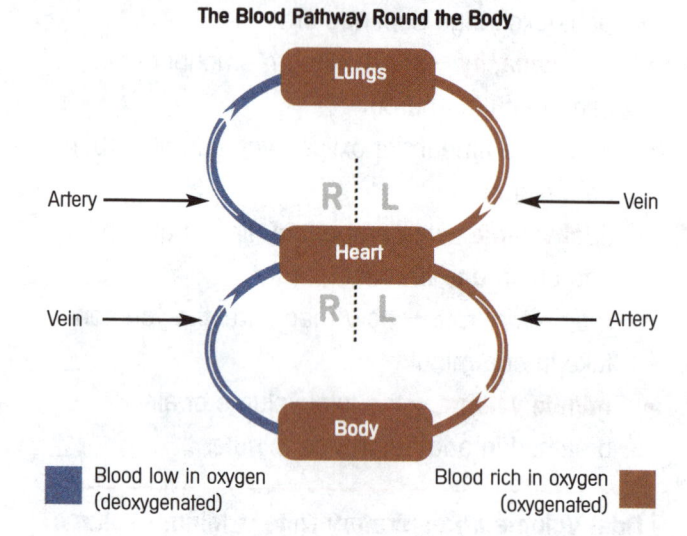

The Blood Pathway Round the Body

■ Blood low in oxygen (deoxygenated)   ■ Blood rich in oxygen (oxygenated)

The Heart

The heart is constructed as a **double pump**, made up of **four chambers**. At the top are the two **atria** and below are the two **ventricles**.

The heart works in the following way:
1. The **right atrium** receives blood from the body and pushes it down into the **right ventricle**.
2. The right ventricle, at the bottom, pushes the blood to the **lungs**.
3. The **left atrium** receives the blood from the lungs and pushes it into the **left ventricle**.
4. The left ventricle sends the blood to the **body**.

The ventricles don't beat at exactly the same time. This means that the **pulse beat** is a double beat, although one is slightly stronger than the other.

Superior **vena cava**, (main vein taking back blood with little oxygen to the heart)

Aorta (main artery carrying oxygen around the body)

Semi-lunar valve stops blood flowing back into ventricle

Pulmonary artery takes back blood with little oxygen to lungs

Right atrium

Left atrium

Tricuspid valve

Pulmonary vein takes back blood with oxygen

Tendons and cords holding valves in place

Mitral valve / Bicuspid stops the blood going back

Inferior vena cava

Bottom right muscular ventricle squeezes blood along to the lungs

An artery

Bottom left very muscular ventricle squeezes blood along aorta to body

Pulse

A pulse beat can only be found in an **artery**. It is a **pressure wave** travelling along the artery. The pulse can be measured wherever an artery is close to the **skin surface**.

The pulse can beat in an irregular manner and is usually measured over a **full minute**. A **pulse rate** should be measured using the finger ends only.

The Usual Places to Measure the Pulse

Radial artery at the wrist

Carotid artery at the neck

Femoral artery in the groin

Circulatory System

Blood Vessels

Blood vessels form two pathways:
- The **pulmonary pathway** or circuit carries blood from the heart to the lungs and back to the heart.
- The **systemic pathway** or circuit carries blood from the heart to the body and back to the heart.

Arteries carry blood **away** from the heart. They have **thick elastic walls** and become **narrower** as they get further from the heart.

Veins carry blood **back** to the heart. They have thinner, **less elastic walls**. The **closer** to the heart they are, the **thicker** they are.

Capillaries are very fine, thin blood vessels that join the ends of the arteries to the ends of the veins. They're **very narrow**, only wide enough to allow **single blood cells** to pass through one at a time. Their walls are **one cell thick**. Gas exchange takes place through these walls.

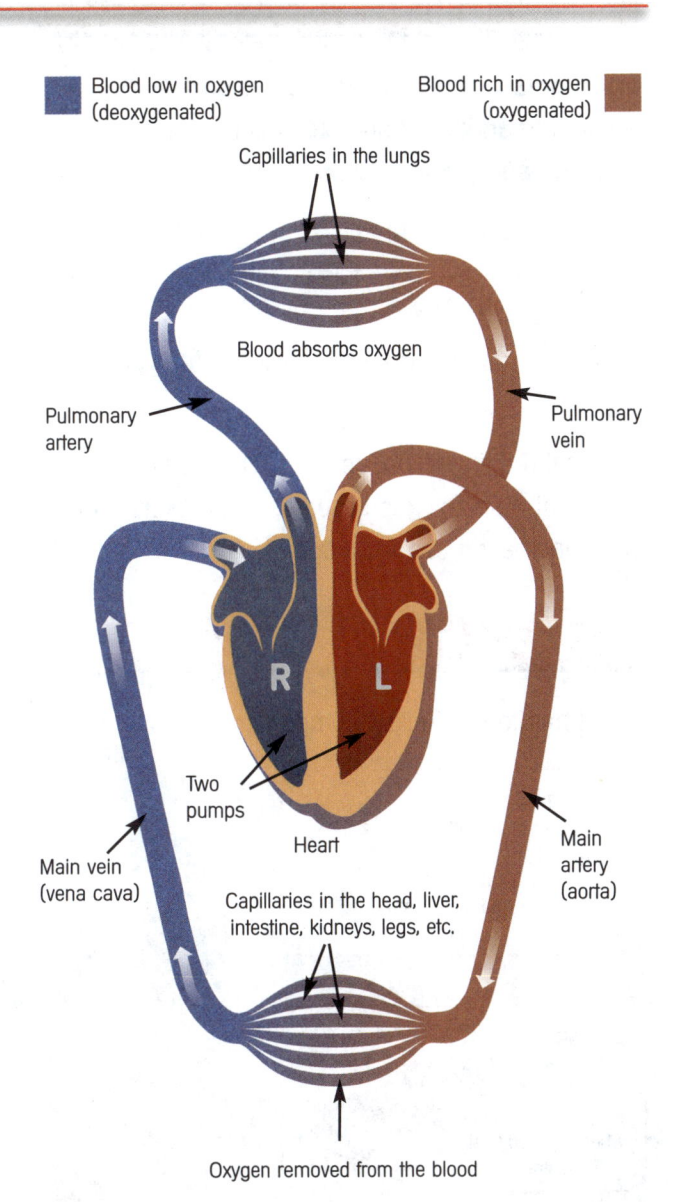

Blood low in oxygen (deoxygenated)
Blood rich in oxygen (oxygenated)

Capillaries in the lungs
Blood absorbs oxygen
Pulmonary artery
Pulmonary vein
R L
Two pumps
Heart
Main vein (vena cava)
Main artery (aorta)
Capillaries in the head, liver, intestine, kidneys, legs, etc.
Oxygen removed from the blood

Quick Test

1. What are the top two chambers of the heart called?
2. Where does the systemic circuit carry blood to?
3. Which vessel carries blood from the lungs to the heart?
4. What is the biggest main artery called?

KEY WORDS

Make sure you understand these words before moving on!
- Circulatory system
- Atria
- Ventricle
- Vena cava
- Tricuspid valve
- Mitral valve
- Artery
- Pulse rate
- Pulmonary pathway
- Systemic pathway
- Vein
- Capillary

Blood Pressure

Measuring Blood Pressure

Blood pressure is measured by using either a **sphygmomanometer** and **stethoscope** or a more modern **battery-powered meter**.

Two measurements are taken:
- **Systolic pressure** – this is when the ventricles **contract**.
- **Diastolic pressure** – this is when the ventricles **relax**.

A typical reading might be 120/80 for a normal person at rest. This increases during exercise due to the increased cardiac output.

A Sphygmomanometer and Stethoscope

Blood and its Functions

Blood has four principal components:

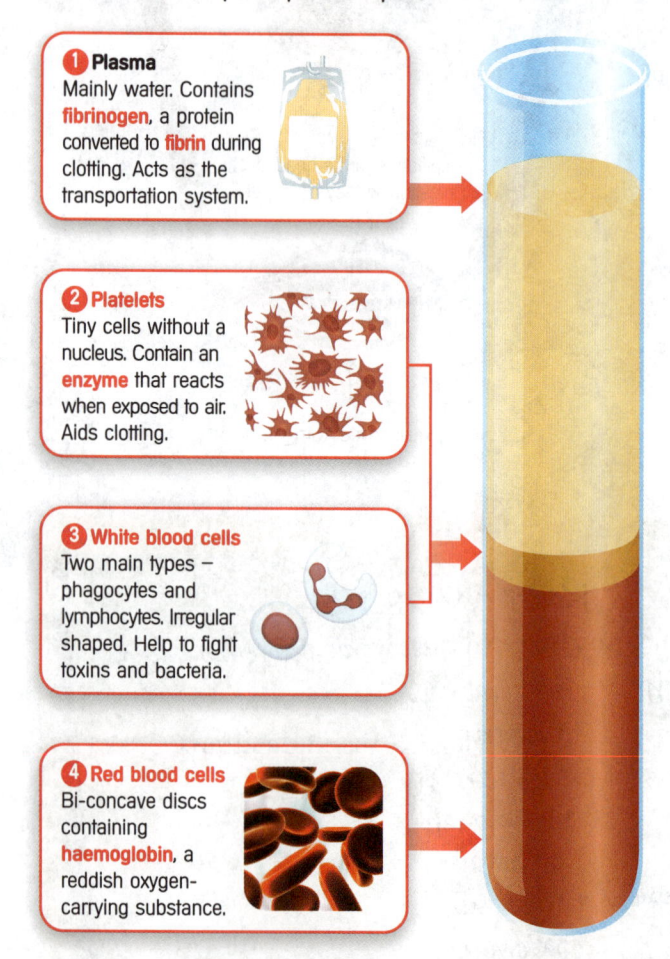

1 Plasma
Mainly water. Contains **fibrinogen**, a protein converted to **fibrin** during clotting. Acts as the transportation system.

2 Platelets
Tiny cells without a nucleus. Contain an **enzyme** that reacts when exposed to air. Aids clotting.

3 White blood cells
Two main types – phagocytes and lymphocytes. Irregular shaped. Help to fight toxins and bacteria.

4 Red blood cells
Bi-concave discs containing **haemoglobin**, a reddish oxygen-carrying substance.

The main functions of blood are **transportation** and **protection**.

Materials Transported by the Blood	
O_2	From the lungs to all body parts
CO_2	From all tissue to lungs
Nutrients	From intestines to all body parts
Heat	From muscles to the body surface
Waste products	From all body tissue to kidneys

Body Protection by the Blood	
Antitoxins	Produced by lymphocytes to fight **toxins** (poisons) that enter the body.
Antibodies	Produced by lymphocytes to fight disease; stay in the bloodstream, give immunity to some illnesses.
Destruction	This is done by phagocytes, which 'eat' harmful organisms.
Clotting	Activated by platelets, which make fibrinogen that forms a **mesh** over the wounded vessel.
Repair	**Nutrients** are taken to the site of damaged tissue to repair it, whether it is broken skin or bone.

Effects of Exercise

Long-Term Effects of Exercise

The **long-term effects** of exercise on the **heart**:
- **Size** and **strength** increase as efficiency improves.
- **Stroke volume** is increased.
- **Cardiac output** is increased.
- **Resting heart** rate becomes lower.
- Return to resting rate after exercise is achieved more quickly.
- The onset of coronary and arterial disease can be prevented.

The **long-term effects** of exercise on the **blood**:
- The number of red cells increases.
- The transportation of oxygen to the muscles is improved.
- The return of carbon dioxide away from the muscles to the lungs is improved.
- The supply to the **muscle fibres** is improved as more capillaries are made ready for work.
- The return of **deoxygenated** blood to the heart is improved.

Short Term Effects of Exercise

The **short-term effects** of exercise on the **heart**:
- **Pulse rate increases**, especially during long-term physical activity.
- **Blood pressure increases**.

The **short-term effects** of exercise on the **blood**:
- More blood is brought into use.
- Blood is **diverted** from the soft organs to the **muscles**.
- Blood **rises** to the surface of the skin, making you look red.
- Blood transports **heat** from the muscles to the body's surface.

Quick Test

1. What is the main part of plasma?
2. What happens to blood pressure during exercise?
3. Where are phagocytes found?
4. What is the long-term effect of exercise on cardiac output?
5. What is the immediate effect of exercise on the pulse rate?

KEY WORDS

Make sure you understand these words before moving on!
- Systolic pressure
- Diastolic pressure
- Fibrinogen
- Fibrin
- Platelets
- Enzyme
- White blood cells
- Red blood cells
- Haemoglobin

Practice Questions

1 Give the anatomical name for each of the following body parts.

   a) Kneecap _____   **b)** Breast bone _____

   c) Shin _____   **d)** Thigh bone _____

2 Give the **four** main functions of the skeleton.

   a) _____   **b)** _____

   c) _____   **d)** _____

3 Name the **five** sections of the vertebral column.

   a) _____   **b)** _____   **c)** _____

   d) _____   **e)** _____

4 a) What attaches bone to bone?

_____

   b) What attaches muscle to bone?

_____

5 a) What happens at a joint when flexion occurs?

_____

_____

   b) What happens at a joint when abduction occurs?

_____

_____

6 Where in the lungs does gas exchange take place?

_____

7 What happens to the diaphragm and the ribs during expiration?

_____

_____

Practice Questions

8 There are three main types of muscle tissue. Give their names and where each of them may be found in the body.

Type of Muscle Tissue	Where it is Found in the Body
a)	
b)	
c)	

9 a) List the **four** principal components of blood.

i) .... ii) ....

iii) .... iv) ....

b) Which of these…

i) transports oxygen? ....

ii) fights toxins and bacteria? ....

10 Draw a diagram showing the circulation of blood around the body and the position of the heart. Label the heart's chambers, using arrows to indicate the pathway that blood flows.

Reasons for Exercise

Why Do Exercise?

People take part in exercise…
- to promote and improve **health** and **fitness**
- to obtain **social benefits**
- to obtain **mental benefits**
- to obtain **physical benefits**.

Social Benefits

Social benefits can be gained from exercise:
- Taking part can help you **meet people**.
- Involvement in team sports helps to develop **team spirit**.
- Involvement can improve **teamwork** and **cooperation** with others.
- **Post-match activities** can be as rewarding as the sport itself.
- Some sports carry **enhanced social status**.
- Sport can improve your image and possibly **earn you money**.

Mental Benefits

Mental benefits can be gained from exercise:
- You get a **challenge** or **goal** to aim for.
- Exercise helps you deal with **stress and tension**.
- Exercise can provide mental as well as physical stimulation.
- Exercise helps you **feel better about yourself** and increases **self-confidence**.
- Exercise helps you look at life with a **better perspective**.
- Exercise can be **fun**.

Reasons for Exercise

Physical Benefits

The **physical benefits** of exercise include…
- an improved **body shape**
- a **good posture**
- the ability to develop **muscle tone**
- **stronger bones**
- the ability to **fight illness and injury**.

Physical benefits contribute to a person's **physical well-being** and **physical fitness**. Fitness…
- is the ability to perform physical activity **efficiently**
- includes physical fitness and motor fitness.

Changes Observed During Physical Activity

	At Rest	During Activity
Depth of Breathing	8 litres / min	25 litres / min
Pulse Rate	75 beats / min	190+ beats / min
Stroke Volume	100 ml / min	200 ml / min
Cardiac Output *	7 litres / min	35+ litres / min
O_2 Used	250 ml / min	4500 ml / min
Size of O_2 Debt Developed	none	10+ litres / min

* Volume of blood pumped out by left ventricle in one minute.

Physical Fitness

Physical fitness is the ability to meet the physical demands of a sporting activity. It has five major components, the 5 Ss:
- Strength
- Speed
- Stamina
- Suppleness
- Somatotype (body composition).

Quick Test
1. What two aspects does exercise promote?
2. By how much does the stroke volume increase during activity?
3. What happens to the pulse rate during activity?
4. What does somatotype mean?
5. True or false – physical benefits do not contribute to a person's physical well-being.

KEY WORDS
Make sure you understand these words before moving on!
- Body shape
- Muscle tone
- Strength
- Speed
- Stamina
- Suppleness
- Somatotype

Reasons for Exercise

The 5 Components of Physical Fitness

1. There are three types of **strength**:
   - **Static** – a **maximum force** against an **immovable object**.
   - **Explosive** – **maximum force** in **one movement**.
   - **Dynamic** – **repeated application** of the **same force**.
2. **Speed** is the **shortest time** taken to move a body, or body part, a **specific distance**.
3. **Stamina** is the ability to perform **strenuous activity** over a **long period of time**, sometimes called **cardiovascular fitness** or **muscular endurance**. For stamina activities, a **continuous supply** of O_2 is needed for the muscles to work.
4. **Suppleness** is the range of movement possible at a joint or joints. This is sometimes referred to as **flexibility** or **mobility**.
5. **Somatotype** is often referred to as **body composition**. The size and shape of a person will affect their ability to perform in individual circumstances.

	Static	Explosive	Dynamic
Activity example	Tug of war, rugby scrum	Shot put, high jump	Rowing, 100m sprint
Body State	Stays the same	Moves fast	Moves fast
Distance Moved	Little or none	Little	Can be considerable
Time Taken	Varies, but not long	Small amount	Can be considerable
Muscle State	Stays the same	Changes quickly	Changes quickly and repeatedly

Aerobic and Anaerobic Fitness

Physical activities require a combination of …
- **aerobic** fitness, for **low intensity** activities lasting a **long** period of time – these activities get their energy demands from **oxygen**
- **anaerobic** fitness, for **higher intensity** activities lasting a **short** period of time – these activities get their energy from **glucose**.

All activities get their energy requirements in varying degrees from **both** these sources.

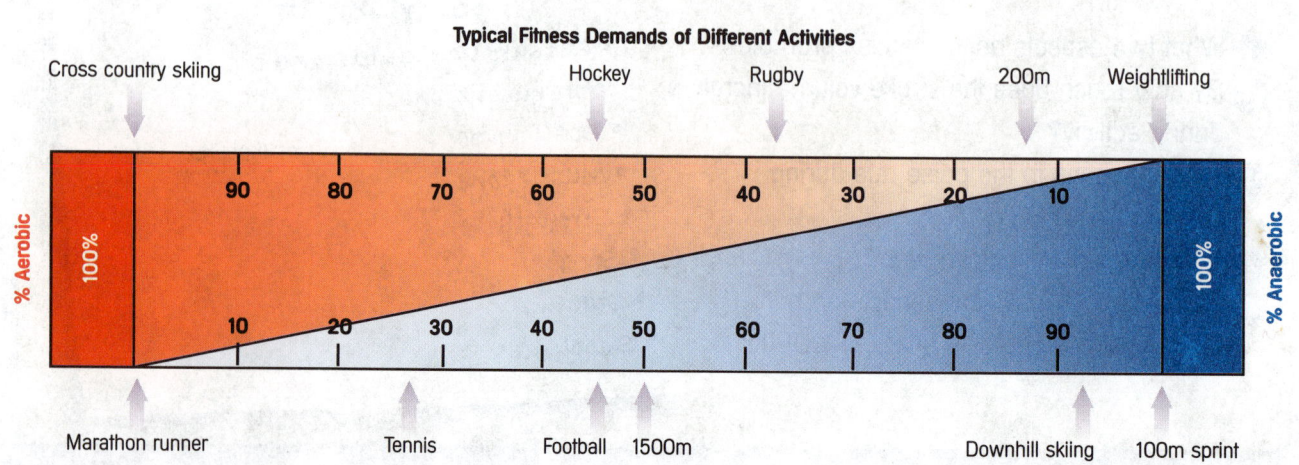

Typical Fitness Demands of Different Activities

Cross country skiing — Hockey — Rugby — 200m — Weightlifting

Marathon runner — Tennis — Football — 1500m — Downhill skiing — 100m sprint

% Aerobic: 100%, 90, 80, 70, 60, 50, 40, 30, 20, 10
% Anaerobic: 10, 20, 30, 40, 50, 60, 70, 80, 90, 100%

Reasons for Exercise

Motor Fitness

Motor fitness is the ability to perform successfully in a given sporting activity. It has six major components:
- **Power** – speed and strength working **together**, as in the shot put.
- **Agility** – the ability to **change direction quickly and accurately**, as in the dodging run.
- **Coordination** – the ability to **perform several tasks**, each linked together, as in a tennis serve or hurdling.
- **Balance** – an **awareness of the body position** at any given time, as in a gymnastic activity on the beam.
- **Reaction** – the **time taken to respond** to a given stimulus, such as responding to the starting pistol at the start of a race.
- **Attitude** – the **psychological approach** of the performer, for example, the will to win, determination.

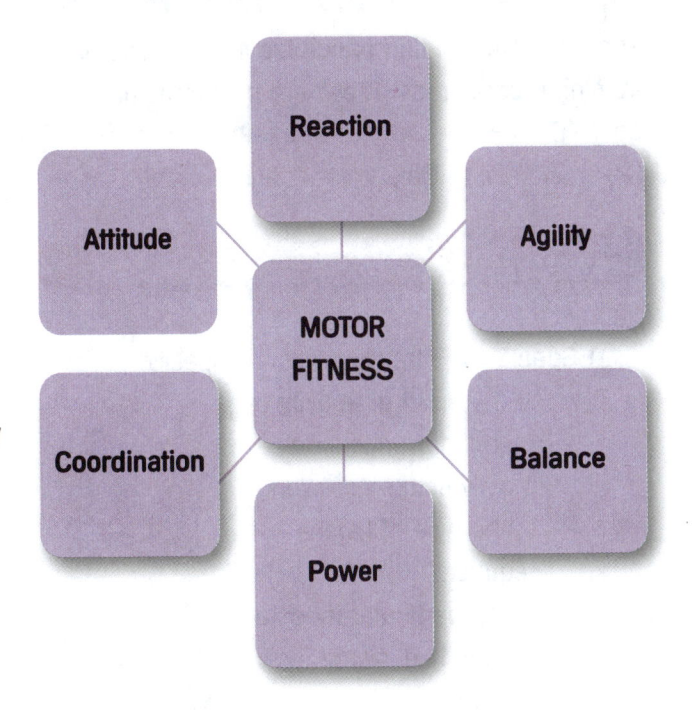

Posture

Exercise improves **muscle tone** around the **vertebrae**. This contributes to **good posture**, which…
- **avoids strain** at joints
- ensures all body parts are **correctly aligned**
- puts **less strain** on other muscles and joints
- helps **avoid deformity**
- helps in **breathing**
- helps **improve flexibility**.

Quick Test

1. What is the ability to change direction quickly and accurately called?
2. What is the other name for cardiovascular fitness and muscular endurance?
3. What is the energy source for anaerobic activities?
4. What is a combination of strength and speed called?

KEY WORDS
Make sure you understand these words before moving on!
- Speed
- Suppleness
- Somatotype
- Aerobic
- Anaerobic
- Agility
- Coordination
- Balance
- Reaction
- Attitude

Principles of Training

Guiding Principles

There are **five guiding principles** that apply to all training programmes. These are best remembered as 'SPORT' – **Specificity**, **Progression**, **Overload**, **Reversibility** and Deterioration, and **Tedium**.

The SPORT Principles

1 Specificity – training must be specific…
- to the **sport or activity** (e.g. marathon runners do mostly endurance work)
- to the **type of fitness** required
- to the **particular muscle groups** (e.g. swimmers exercise specific muscles).

2 Progression – as the body adapts to training it progresses to a **new fitness level**, achieved by a **gradual increase in intensity** to create an **overload**. A typical graph of **levels of fitness** against **time** would look like the graph below.

The graph shows three important points:
- **Most progress** is made in the **early stages**.
- At **higher levels of fitness** there's **less progress**.
- A **plateau** may be reached where **further progression is difficult** to achieve.

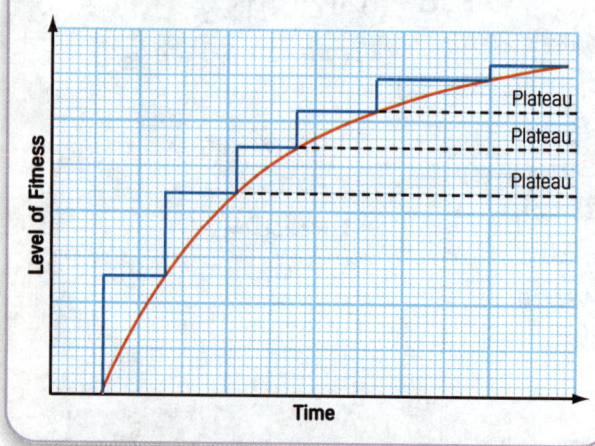

3 Overload – training must be raised to a higher level than normal to create **extra demands** to which the body will adapt. This can be done in four ways:
- **Increasing frequency**, e.g. training more often, three or four times a week.
- **Increasing intensity**, e.g. running faster or lifting heavier weights.
- **Increasing duration** (time), e.g. training longer to prolong demands.
- Changing the **type of exercise** to suit workload.

FITT is an easy way to remember the first and second guiding principles:
- **F** – **frequency** (how often you exercise)
- **I** – **intensity** (how hard you exercise)
- **T** – **time** (how long you exercise for)
- **T** – **type** (which exercises are suitable to your chosen sport)

4 Reversibility – training effects are **reversible**. If exercise is reduced in intensity or stopped altogether, the benefits can be **quickly lost**. Benefits are lost quicker than they're gained.

Deterioration sets in after about **one week**. Strength and speed are **gradually lost** and muscles lose their tone and size. This is **atrophy**.

5 Tedium – training can get **boring**. A **variety of training methods** helps to avoid boredom.

Goal Setting

Setting Targets in Training

Setting **goals** helps to…
- attain **success**
- show **progress**
- show that **planning** is effective
- increase **self-confidence**.

Long-term goals are made up of intermediate and short-term goals.

Goal setting should be **SMART**. Each goal should be a target you aim to reach.

S	SPECIFIC	Decide exactly **what** is to be achieved
M	MEASURABLE	Assess if **progress** is being made
A	AGREED / ACHIEVABLE	Set **targets** with coach / trainer
R	REALISTIC / RECORDED	Ensure goals are **within reach** and **accurate records** are kept
T	TIME-PHASED	**Plan the time** in which you expect to attain **specific goals**

Motivation

Motivation is how keen you are to attain your set goals. There are two kinds of motivation:

1. **Intrinsic motivation**…
   - comes from **inside you**
   - reflects your **will to win**.
2. **Extrinsic motivation**…
   - comes from **outside you** and **spurs you on**
   - can come in the form of **rewards or prizes**.

The graph shows how **arousal** affects motivation:
- **Too little** arousal leads to **poor performance** (**A**).
- **Too much** arousal can lead to **nerves and stress**, which can affect performance (**C**).
- If the arousal level is **just right** then performance will be at its **best** (**B**).

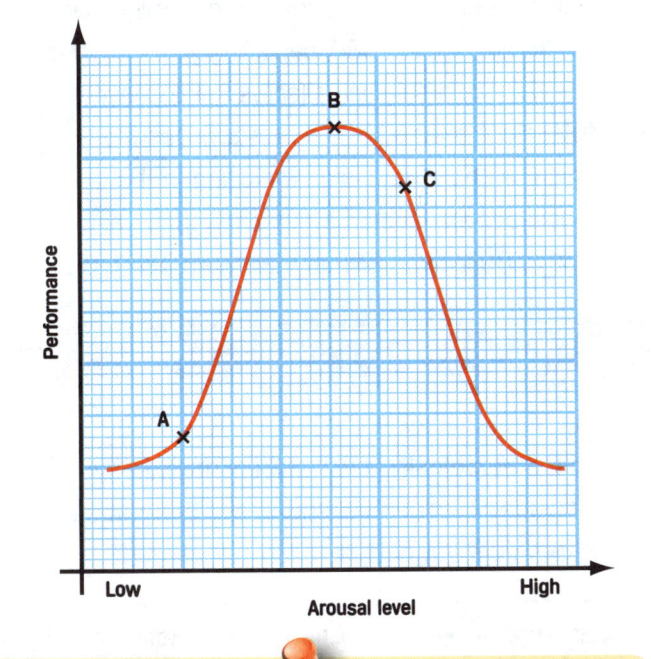

Quick Test

1. What does FITT stand for?
2. What are the four ways in which overload can be attained?
3. How long does it take for deterioration to set in?
4. What does the M in SMART stand for?
5. What are the two types of motivation?

KEY WORDS
Make sure you understand these words before moving on!
- Specificity
- Progression
- Overload
- Reversibility
- Tedium
- Goals
- Motivation
- Arousal

Training Threshold

Worthwhile Training

For training to be **worthwhile work** it must be…
- **strenuous**
- **effective**.

If the **work rate** is **too high** then…
- **injury** can be caused
- **oxygen debt** will develop.

A **training threshold** rate (TTR) is…
- a **safe level** to work at
- an **effective level** to work at
- work done **aerobically**.

There are several ways an individual can work out their TTR:
- **180 method** – assuming that the maximum heart rate for all people is 180, deducting your age from 180 will give a safe and effective training level.
- **70%–80% method** – this presupposes the maximum heart rate is as indicated in the table opposite. It's based on a person working at 70% to 80% of a notional maximum heart rate.
- **60% method** – this adds 60% of the range of your heart rate to your resting rate.
- **Karvonen's formula** – this adds 70% of the range to your resting rate.

These last two methods depend upon the athlete establishing their maximum heart rate. This should only be established under **supervision**.

Age	Max Heart Rate (beats / min)	Safe Working Rate (beats / min)
20	200	140 / 160
30	190	133 / 152
40	180	126 / 144
50	170	119 / 136

The TTR is sometimes referred to as the **target or training zone**. At this level the intensity of effort will be most effective.

Oxygen Debt

Training at or just below the correct TTR will be work done **aerobically**. It will still ensure that the work includes overload but should not bring about an **oxygen debt** (O_2 debt).

Glucose —explosively→ Energy + Lactic acid

Training above the TTR will be work done **anaerobically**, producing an oxygen debt and thus **lactic acid**.

A build-up of lactic acid causes **fatigue**. This acid can only be broken down (removed) by oxygen, i.e. the **repayment of the debt**.

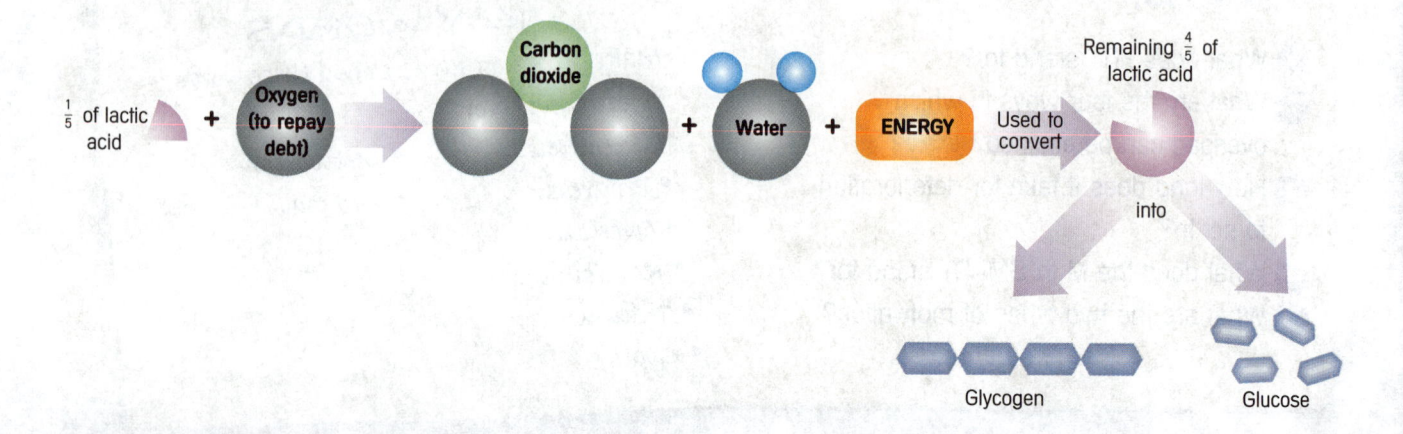

$\frac{1}{5}$ of lactic acid + Oxygen (to repay debt) → Carbon dioxide + Water + ENERGY Used to convert Remaining $\frac{4}{5}$ of lactic acid into Glycogen / Glucose

Aerobic and Anaerobic Training

Aerobic Training

Aerobic training should…
- be **moderately strenuous**
- be **prolonged**
- be carried out at approximately the **TTR level**
- use the **larger muscle groups**.

Aerobic training affects the body by…
- improving breathing – **deeper, fuller** breaths
- increasing chest size
- increasing the heart size (**bradycardia**)
- improving circulation, as more red cells become available for work
- raising the **aerobic threshold**
- improving endurance
- improving cardiovascular fitness
- increasing lung capacity
- bringing about a **lower resting heart rate**
- **reducing the risk** of cardiovascular disease.

Anaerobic Training

Anaerobic training should…
- be **very strenuous**
- be done in **short bursts**
- be done **above** the TTR level
- include **rest and recovery periods**
- be undertaken with **caution**.

Anaerobic training affects the body by…
- raising the **anaerobic threshold**
- improving muscular strength
- improving **lactic acid tolerance**
- increasing the ability to use the body's **fat stores** for energy
- increasing muscle size (**hypertrophy**).

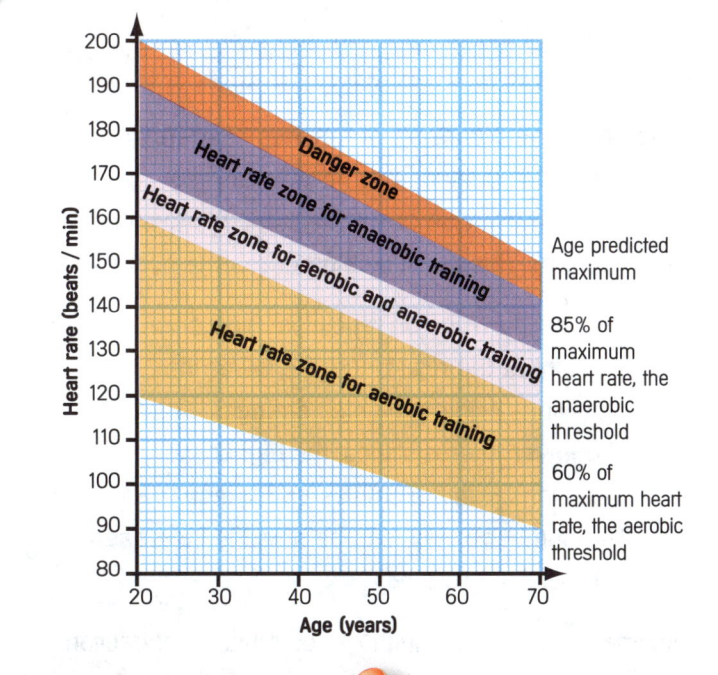

Quick Test

1. What does TTR stand for?
2. What kind of work is done below the TTR?
3. How should maximum heart rate be established?
4. What other quality should aerobic training have as well as being strenuous?
5. What should be included in an anaerobic training session?

KEY WORDS
Make sure you understand these words before moving on!
- Oxygen debt
- Lactic acid
- Fatigue
- Bradycardia
- Aerobic threshold
- Anaerobic threshold

Training Methods

Ways of Training

All training methods…
- place an emphasis on a number of the fitness components
- train both the **aerobic** and **anaerobic** systems
- have **different intensity levels** to suit the needs of the activity
- are **wide ranging** in type
- are to some extent **effective**.

There are several training methods and they…
- all consist of activities that need to be **organised**
- are organised into **repetitions** or **sets**.

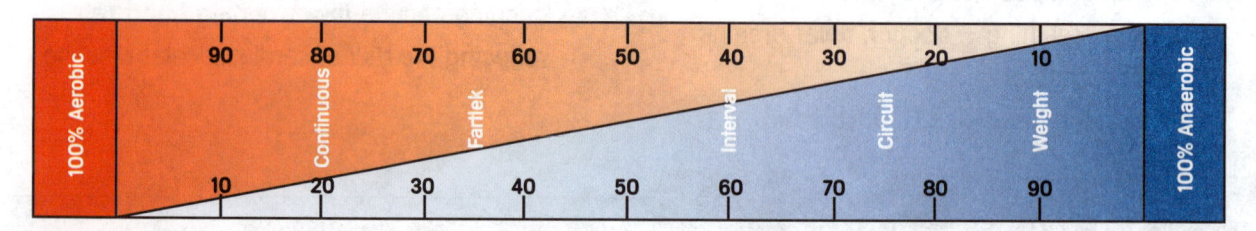

100% Aerobic	90	80	70	60	50	40	30	20	10	100% Anaerobic
	Continuous		Fartlek			Interval		Circuit	Weight	
	10	20	30	40	50	60	70	80	90	

Weight Training

Weight training consists of a **series of exercises**. Each exercise puts focus on a **different muscle group**. Each exercise has a **resistance** to overcome (the weight). This resistance produces the **overload**.

Weight training relies on repetitions and sets:
- The **higher** the resistance, the **lower** the repetitions – this promotes **strength**.
- The **lower** the resistance, the **higher** the repetitions – this promotes **endurance**.
- The number of sets can be **steadily increased** to **raise the overload**.

Isometric weight training is when muscle contraction **does not** produce movement. The **load** is held for approximately 5 seconds before relaxation. This **develops strength** rather than endurance.

Isotonic weight training is when muscle contraction **does** produce movement. Movement is repeated and rapid. This develops both stamina and strength.

Weight training can improve the performance of skills and…
- improve **muscular strength** and **endurance**
- improve **muscle tone** and **posture**
- increase **muscular size** and **bone density**
- increase **metabolic rate**.

For Strength
10 Reps
3 Sets
Large Load

For Endurance
20 Reps
3 Sets
Small Load

Training Methods

Circuit Training

Circuit training is a series of activities, one after the other. Circuits are of two types.

Fitness circuits put the emphasis on aspects of fitness. Each exercise concentrates on a **different** body part. Exercises are arranged so that alternate parts receive emphasis. Overall the body receives a **balanced distribution of work**.

Skills circuits are designed to improve the skills of a specific game. The skills take the place of exercises.

Advantages of circuit training:
- The **variety of exercises** prevents boredom.
- Any kind of exercise can be included.
- It's easy to **measure progress**.
- Circuits can be organised for **indoor** or **outdoor use**.

Circuits can be organised in two ways.

1. **Fixed load**:
   - Each exercise is performed continually for a given time with rest periods between each.
   - To increase overload, work periods are **lengthened and rest periods shortened**.

2. **Individual load**:
   - The individual establishes their own level of work, i.e. 50% to 60% of their maximum in one minute.
   - The circuit is then performed **continuously** and is **timed**.
   - Rest periods come on completion of each circuit.
   - To increase overload, circuit times must be improved on, the level of work can be **increased** and the length of rest periods can be **reduced**.

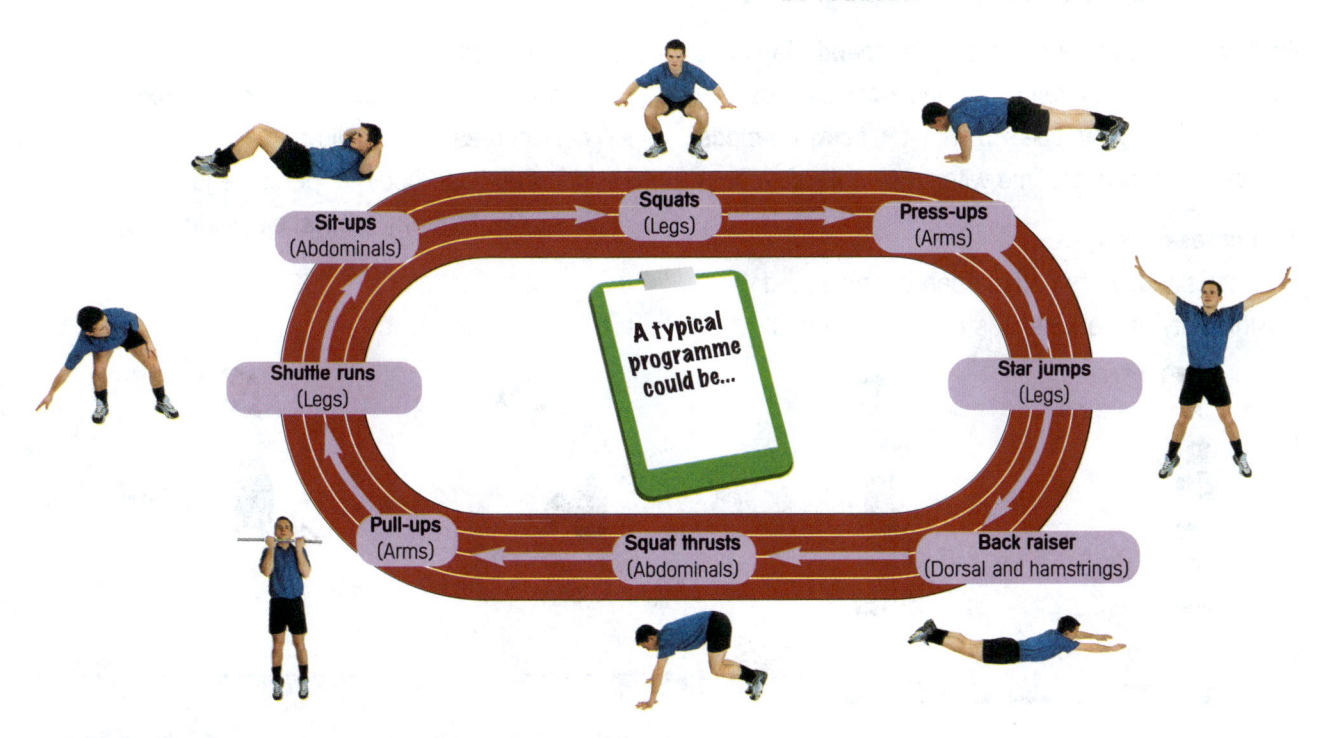

A typical programme could be...

- Sit-ups (Abdominals)
- Squats (Legs)
- Press-ups (Arms)
- Star jumps (Legs)
- Back raiser (Dorsal and hamstrings)
- Squat thrusts (Abdominals)
- Pull-ups (Arms)
- Shuttle runs (Legs)

Effects of Circuit Training

Circuit training can **improve**…
- strength and endurance
- muscle tone and posture
- skill level.

Circuit training can **increase** bone density and metabolic rate, and can **decrease** body-fat percentage.

Training Methods

Interval Training

Training methods that involve running are the most well known and effective. Interval training alternates between fixed periods of **work** and of **rest** or **recovery** **time**.

To increase the load…

- **duration** of work time can be increased
- **intensity** of work can be increased
- **number** of work periods can be increased
- rest or recovery times can be reduced.

This type of training…

- makes it **easy to measure progress**
- requires little equipment
- improves both aerobic and anaerobic fitness
- increases metabolic rate
- decreases body fat percentage
- is most suited to team sports, running and swimming.

25m sprint → 30 sec rest → 25m sprint → 30 sec rest …and so on

Fartlek Training

Fartlek (a Swedish word meaning '**speed play**') is a form of continuous training. It has **work periods** of **varying intensity** interspersed with **low activity periods** and provides recovery time with low activity periods.

To **increase the load**…

- intensity of work periods can be increased
- intensity of work periods can be extended.

This type of training…

- can **improve both aerobic and anaerobic fitness**
- can increase metabolic rate
- can decrease body fat percentage
- is **suited to many sports**, e.g. swimming.

10 min jog → 100m walk → 50m sprint → 5 min jog …and so on

Continuous Training

Continuous training is long, slow, distance (LSD) running at a **constant rate without rest periods**, at approximately **60% of maximum heart rate**.

To **increase the load**…

- the level of intensity can be increased
- distance can be increased.

This type of training…

- improves aerobic fitness
- increases metabolic rate
- decreases body fat percentage
- is **most suited to aerobic activities**, e.g. marathons.

Training Methods

Flexibility Training

Flexibility training is a series of mobility exercises at specific joints. The emphasis is on **increasing the range of movement** at joints.

Each joint is stretched to just beyond the **point of resistance**. The stretch should be held for approximately 8 to 10 seconds and they should be carried out at least three times a week to be effective.

Types of flexibility stretching are…

- **passive static stretching** – a **partner** moving the joint **beyond its point of resistance**
- **active static stretching** – the **performer** moving the joint **beyond its point of resistance**
- **ballistic stretching** – using **body momentum** to **stretch the joint**, e.g. arm swinging and twisting.

The **advantages of flexibility training** are that it's cheap and easy to do, needs little equipment, and supports playing a wide range of activities.

Active Static Stretching (hips)

Active Static Stretching (back)

Passive Static Stretching (back)

Ballistic Stretching (side)

Quick Test

1. What does interval training alternate between?
2. What does LSD stand for?
3. What does Fartlek mean?
4. What does ballistic stretching use?
5. What are exercises organised into?
6. What provides the resistance in weight training?

KEY WORDS
Make sure you understand these words before moving on!
- Aerobic
- Anaerobic
- Intensity level
- Repetitions
- Sets
- Muscle groups
- Resistance
- Overload
- Load
- Fixed load
- Rest
- Individual load
- Recovery
- Flexibility
- Passive stretching
- Active stretching

Programmes of Exercise

Exercise Programmes

Although not strictly training methods, there are a number of **exercise programmes** that benefit the individual. They all, to some extent...
- help to **promote fitness**
- concentrate on the **fun** aspect of exercise
- tend not to need much equipment
- concentrate on a number of specific fitness components.

Aerobic Programmes

Aerobics develops **cardiovascular fitness**:
- It aims to improve muscle tone and reduce body fat percentage.
- It consists of a **set pattern** of **continuous aerobic exercises**.
- It's performed without equipment and often to music.
- Classes can be large or small and follow a leader's directions.
- Rest periods reflect the intensity of the session.

Step aerobics is related to aerobics but includes a single piece of equipment, a portable step. The step is freestanding and can be approached from any side.

Exercises include stepping on and off in time to the music. Intensity can be introduced to this activity as the steps can be adjusted in height. This lifting of body weight can be very demanding.

Aqua aerobics is another aerobics-related activity but this takes place in a swimming pool. Exercises are similar to the conventional aerobics programme but with the constraints that water imposes.

The exercises are good for overweight people and those recovering from illness and injury, as the water supports the body weight during exercise.

Body Conditioning Programmes

Pilates is a body conditioning programme. It includes **stretch and mobility work** with **static strength exercises**. Injuries rarely occur owing to the level of intensity.

Pilates combines **physical work** with a **philosophical approach** that promotes the feel good, look good factor.

Yoga is a conditioning programme that aims to unify **physical performance** with a **mental approach**.

Yoga includes **passive stretching activities** combined with **mobility work** and some **static strength work**.

Progress is achieved through carefully structured **intensity levels** to improve vitality, stamina, posture, strength and weight reduction.

Training Requirements

Seasonal Sports

Seasonal sports take place at a **specific time of year**. This allows training to be scheduled into four main sections:

- **Closed** or **off season** – for rest, relaxation and recovery.
- **Out of season** training – for aerobic and strength training, and preparing the body.
- **Pre-season** training – for more intense fitness work and any skills training needed.
- **Playing season** – to maintain fitness levels and to reflect times of competitions.

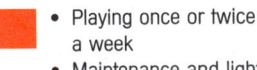

- Playing once or twice a week
- Maintenance and light weight training
- Speed work
- Quality rest and appropriate diet

- High intensity interval and weights training
- Flexibility and 'pressure' skills training
- Practice matches

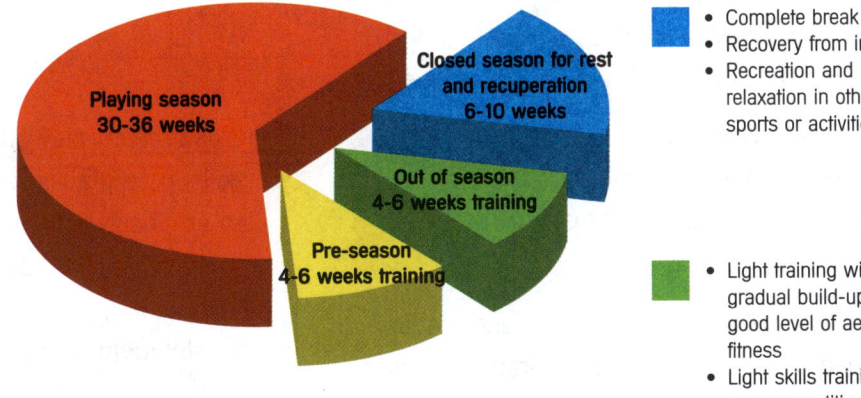

Playing season 30-36 weeks
Closed season for rest and recuperation 6-10 weeks
Out of season 4-6 weeks training
Pre-season 4-6 weeks training

- Complete break
- Recovery from injuries
- Recreation and relaxation in other sports or activities

- Light training with gradual build-up to good level of aerobic fitness
- Light skills training with non-competitive games

Training Venues

Training venues can vary for individual competitors.

For **lower level competitors**…
- training takes place around home, work and club
- outdoor sports may include more indoor work
- activities are usually **self-financed**.

Elite level competitors…
- often look for warm weather or high altitude training venues
- rely on **funding**, **sponsorship** and **self-finance** to make this possible.

Periodisation

Periodisation is the method of organising training within blocks of time. These are training programmes with medium and long-term goals and may extend over several years, e.g. Olympics preparation.

Specific levels of performance are aimed for at specific times of the year. Each level should be higher than the previous one. Preparation periods are included.

Peaking

Training must reflect the competition calendar. **Peaking** aims for a **best performance at a specific time** in the season.

Training intensity needs to be varied throughout the competitive season and it should be planned to achieve peaks that correspond with specific competitions.

Training Sessions

Training Times

Training sessions should be planned in a specific manner and should be...
- **interesting** – include different activities to prevent boredom
- **useful** – to meet the needs of those taking part
- **suitable to the participant** – take account of age, injuries, fitness levels, health problems and physical abilities.

All training sessions should include...
- a **warm-up** phase
- a **fitness** or **exercise** phase
- a **skill** or **team-play** phase
- a **warm-down** (cool down) phase.

Training Phases

The **warm-up** is **essential** as it...
- **prepares the body and mind** for work
- **raises the heart rate** and breathing levels
- reduces the possibility of injury.

The warm-up includes light exercises and mobility work, especially stretches and pulse-raising work and is aimed to complement the main part of the session.

The fitness or exercise phase should...
- include a **selection of different exercises** aimed at one or more fitness components
- **maintain progression** and gradual overload.

The skill or team-play phase should include...
- skills to be practised in small group situations
- an emphasis on the full game
- some conditioned play to emphasise certain types of play
- **development of team skills** and tactics.

The **warm-down** phase is **essential**...
- to allow the body to return to its steady state
- to **return the pulse** to its **normal resting rate**
- to flush out **residual lactic acid**
- to **prevent stiffness** and soreness
- to repay any oxygen debt
- to **remove any extra blood** from the muscles to prevent blood pooling in the veins, which can make the athlete dizzy or weak.

Examples of Stretching Exercises to Warm-up

Effects of Exercise

Long-Term Effects of Exercise

Each body system is affected by exercise and there are several long-term effects.

In the **circulatory system** the…
- heart can get bigger
- resting rate gets slower
- stroke volume and red cell count increase.

In the **respiratory system**…
- the chest becomes larger
- vital capacity increases
- the capillary network increases
- there's improved gas exchange
- oxygen supply and waste removal is improved.

In the **skeletal system**…
- the bones become stronger
- the ligaments become stronger
- articular cartilage can increase.

In the **muscular system**…
- muscles get bigger (**hypertrophy**) and stronger
- more muscle fibres are made ready for work
- tendons become stronger
- flexibility can increase
- the muscles become more resistant to lactic acid build-up
- recovery from injury can be quicker.

Temperature Regulation

The **thermoregulatory centre** in the brain monitors and controls the core temperature of the body to maintain it at around **37 degrees**. The **shunt vessel system** adapts to needs.

In order to maintain core temperature in **hot conditions**…
- blood vessels under the skin **vasodilate** (get bigger)
- the skin surface becomes red
- heat is **radiated** through the **skin surface**
- sweat glands release sweat to **cool the body surface**
- **panting** brings cool air into the body and passes hot air out.

In order to maintain core temperature in **cold conditions**…
- blood vessels under the skin **vasoconstrict** (become narrower)
- heat loss by radiation is reduced
- **muscles shiver**, causing heat to be released via respiration in cells.

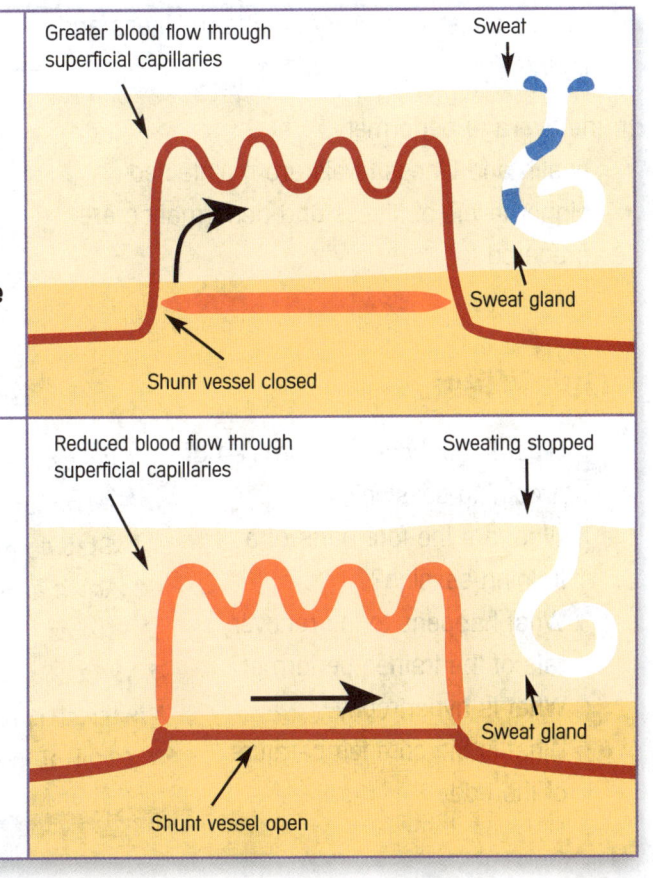

Effects of Exercise

Short-Term Effects of Exercise

Immediate effects of exercise on **respiration** and **muscles**:

- Increased muscle action needs more energy.
- Respiration in muscles increases.
- More oxygen and glucose are used.
- More oxygen and carbon dioxide and some lactic acid is produced.
- Respiratory rate and tidal volume increase.
- Body temperature starts to rise.
- The blood vessels vasodilate.
- The skin becomes flushed.
- Sweat is produced.

Immediate effects of exercise on the **cardiovascular system**:

- Heart rate increases.
- Stroke volume increases.
- Blood flows faster around the body.
- Blood is diverted away from the stomach and intestines and directed to the muscles.
- Blood pressure rises.
- More oxygen is delivered to working muscles more quickly.
- Carbon dioxide and other waste products are removed more quickly.

General Effects of Exercise

The overall effect of exercise on performers varies.

In the **highly trained** performer…

- higher fitness levels are maintained
- **motor skills** become fine tuned
- there's a faster recovery rate
- there's a faster recovery time from illness and injury.

In the **average** performer…

- health and fitness levels are maintained
- higher levels of fitness and performance are prepared for.

In the **below average** performer…

- **basic fitness** levels improve quickly
- heart rate and blood pressure are **lowered**
- **sleep patterns** are improved
- body fat percentage is **reduced**.

Quick Test

1. What should come at the start of a training session?
2. What are the four parts of a training session?
3. What happens to the recovery rate of the trained performer?
4. What is hypertrophy?
5. What is the core temperature of the body?

KEY WORDS

Make sure you understand these words before moving on!

- Aerobics
- Step aerobics
- Aqua aerobics
- Pilates
- Yoga
- Intensity level
- Seasonal sport
- Capillary network
- Thermoregulatory centre
- Shunt vessel system
- Vasodilate
- Respiration
- Cardiovascular system

Testing

Tests for Fitness

All components of training can be **tested**. Pre and post tests can show...
- if **progression** is being made
- if the training method is **effective**.

All tests must measure what they set out to measure – this is called **validity**. All tests should be carried out in the same way every time – this is called **test protocol**. (See Appendix, P90).

Tests of Strength

For **hand and forearm strength**, a **grip dynamometer** is used.

For **leg and back strength**, a **tensiometer** is used.

To measure explosive leg strength (power), the **standing long jump** and **standing high jump** can be used.

Grip dynamometer

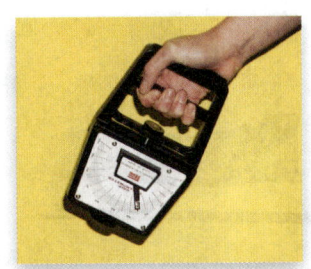

Tensiometer

Standing Long Jump

Standing High Jump

Tests for Suppleness

For mobility at the shoulder, the **shoulder lift test** is used.

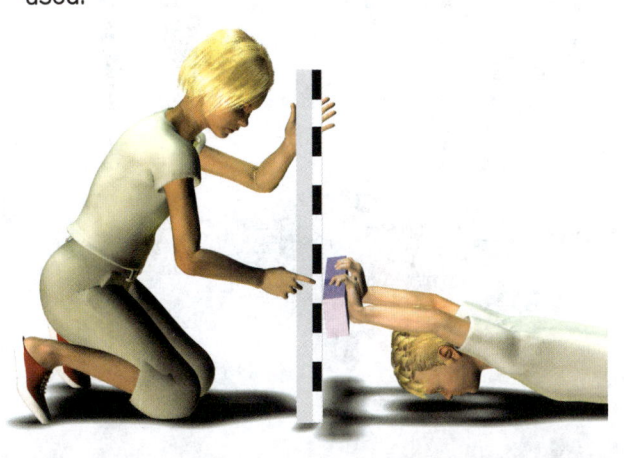

For mobility at the lower back, the **sit-and-reach test** is used.

Testing

Tests for Local Muscular Stamina

Press-ups measure **arm and body strength** as well as **muscular endurance**:

Sit-ups measure the **strength and endurance** of the **stomach muscles**:

Tests for Cardiovascular Fitness

Cardiovascular fitness is referred to as cardiovascular stamina, aerobic power and aerobic capacity.

In the **Harvard step test**, you step on and off a box that's 40cm high for 5 minutes, at a rate of 30 steps per minute.

A fitness rating is obtained using this formula:

$$\frac{100 \ \times \ 300 \text{ (time in seconds)}}{5.5 \ \times \ \text{heart rate at end of test}}$$

This is called a **sub-maximal test** as the activity rate is **pre-determined**.

In the **12-minute run test** (the **Cooper Test**) you run and / or walk as far as possible in 12 minutes. The fitness level is determined by comparing the distance run to established norms. This is described as a **maximal test**.

In the **Progressive shuttle run test** (also described as the bleep test or the multi-stage fitness test), you run between lines 20 metres apart. The pace is decided by bleeps on a tape or disc. When three bleeps are missed, the fitness level is established. This is a maximal test.

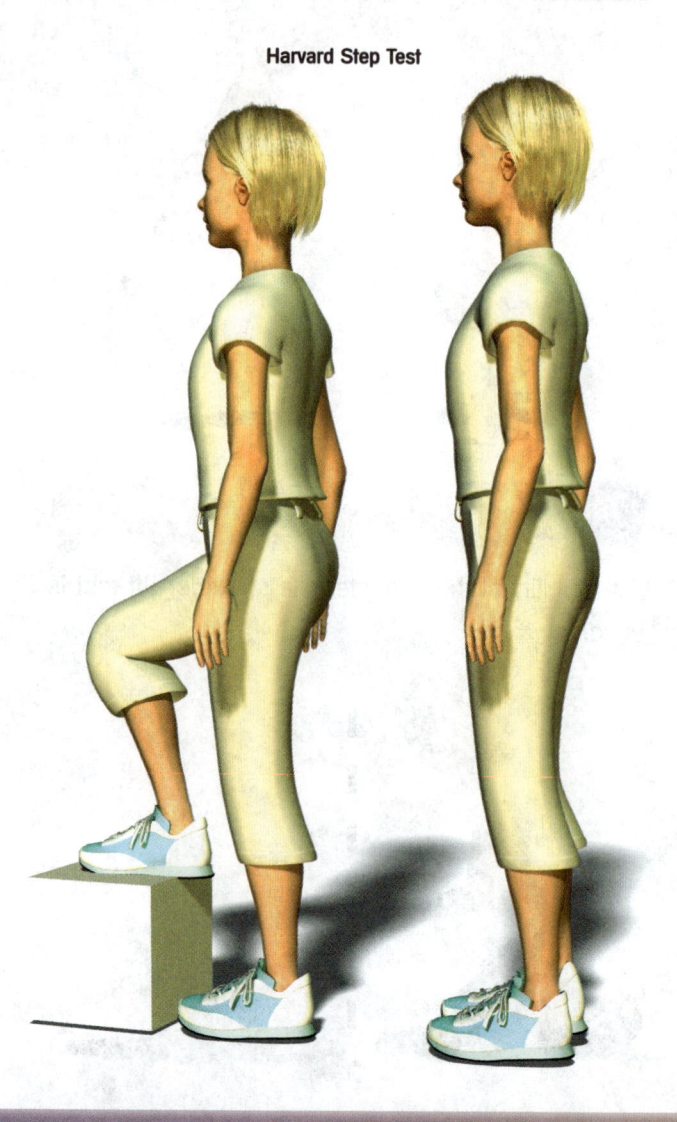

Harvard Step Test

Testing

Tests of Speed and Skill

In a **sprint test** you're timed over an agreed distance. As distances and protocols vary, no norms are given.

The **Illinois Agility Run** is a test for skill-related fitness. **Agility** is a combination of **speed** and **change of direction**. You're timed over a pre-designed pathway under specific protocols. Fitness level is determined from established norms.

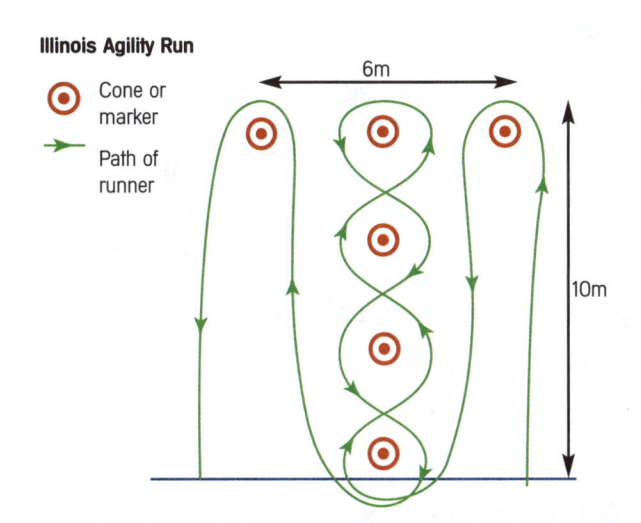

Illinois Agility Run
- Cone or marker
- Path of runner

6m, 10m

Tests for Reaction

In a **rule drop test**, a ruler is dropped without warning and you must catch it as soon as possible.

Measurement is the distance from the bottom of the ruler to the point where the thumb / finger catches the ruler.

Tests for Balance

The **stork stand test** is a test for balance:
1. You stand on one foot.
2. Your other foot is placed against your knee.
3. Hands are placed on **hips**.
4. Timing starts when your eyes close.
5. Timing stops when your eyes open or you lose your balance.

Stork Stand Test

Fitness and Training Practice Questions

1 What three benefits does exercise give you?

   a) .... b) .... c) ....

2 What are the five major components of physical fitness?

   a) .... b) .... c) ....

   d) .... e) ....

3 Explain what the following terms mean.

   a) Static strength

   ....

   b) Explosive strength

   ....

   c) Dynamic strength

   ....

4 Fill in the missing words to complete the following sentences.

   a) Another name for body composition is ....

   b) Aerobic activities get their energy from ....

   c) Anaerobic activities get their energy from ....

5 Goal setting should be SMART. What does SMART stand for?

   S ....

   M ....

   A ....

   R ....

   T ....

6 Fill in the missing word to complete the following sentence.

   When you train anaerobically, the poisonous by-product .... acid is produced.

Fitness and Training Practice Questions

7 Circle the correct option in the following sentence.

Hypertrophy is a(n) **increase / decrease** in muscle size.

8 How much movement takes place during isometric weight training? Tick the correct option.

　A None ◯　　　**B** A little ◯　　　**C** A lot ◯

9 Is the following statement **true** or **false**?

A fixed load circuit is one that is performed for a given time. ....

10 Fill in the missing words to complete the following sentence.

Interval training consists of fixed periods of .... and fixed periods of ....

11 What is speed play also known as?

....

12 Fill in the missing words to complete the following sentences.

　a) Peaking is the .... performance at a .... time.

　b) The long-term effects of exercise on the circulatory system can lead to the heart getting .... and the .... pulse lower. The stroke volume and the .... cell count increase.

13 Give three reasons why a warm-up phase is included in a training session.

　a) ....

　b) ....

　c) ....

14 What tests are used for the following fitness components?

　a) Hand / Forearm strength ....

　b) Mobility at the lower back ....

　c) Agility ....

　d) Balance ....

Factors Affecting Performance

Physique

Physique is often referred to as **body shape** or **somatotype**. Different body shapes suit different sports. Physique is measured on three **seven-point scales**, which we all have some features of:

Mesomorph	Ectomorph	Endomorph
Very muscular	Very thin	Very fat
Large head	Narrow face, high forehead	Fatty upper arms
Broad shoulders	Narrow shoulders	Narrow shoulders
Strong forearms and thighs	Thin, narrow chest and abdomen	Relatively thin wrists. Fatty thighs
Narrow hips	Slim hips	Wide hips

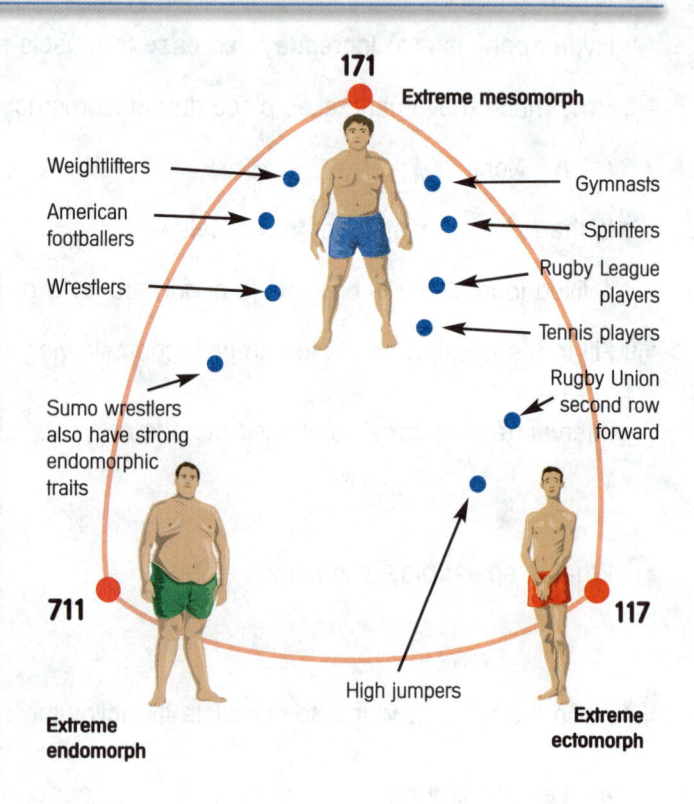

171 Extreme mesomorph
- Weightlifters
- American footballers
- Wrestlers
- Gymnasts
- Sprinters
- Rugby League players
- Tennis players
- Rugby Union second row forward

Sumo wrestlers also have strong endomorphic traits

711 Extreme endomorph

High jumpers

117 Extreme ectomorph

Age and Gender

Age affects performance:
- In formative or younger years, performance levels can be **higher**.
- As we get older, performance levels **decrease**.
- In later years, performance levels are at their **lowest**.

Gender affects performance. There's little difference between the sexes until puberty is reached, when significant changes occur.

During **male puberty**...
- testosterone makes boys **bigger** and **stronger**
- strength to weight ratio increases
- bigger muscles and bones develop
- weight increases; the heart and lungs become larger.

During **female puberty**...
- the pelvis becomes wider for future **childbirth**
- **flexibility** is more pronounced
- a higher percentage of body fat is maintained
- the onset of **menstruation** can affect body weight and thus performance.

Influence of Age on Performance

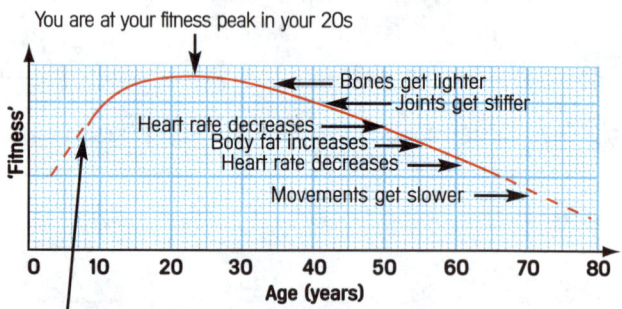

You are at your fitness peak in your 20s
- Bones get lighter
- Joints get stiffer
- Heart rate decreases
- Body fat increases
- Heart rate decreases
- Movements get slower

Formative years. Skill levels develop through a variety of experiences and the ingraining of 'good habits', e.g. regular practice.

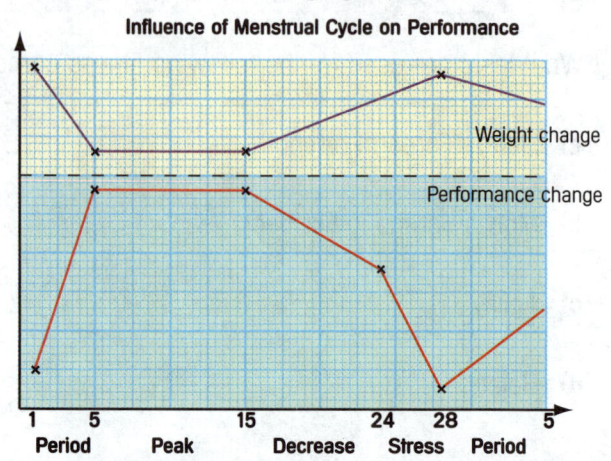

Influence of Menstrual Cycle on Performance

- Weight change
- Performance change

1–5 Period | Peak | 15 Decrease | 24–28 Stress | 5 Period

Factors Affecting Performance

Environment

The **environment** you live or exercise in can affect performance:

- At **altitude** the air is **thinner** with **lower oxygen levels**. This can enhance power for anaerobic events but hinder endurance events.
- **Weather differentials** such as wind, rain, heat and cold can affect training and performance. **High** and **low humidity** can affect temperature regulation and dehydration.
- **Pollution** can affect the functions of the respiratory system, making aerobic / endurance events harder.

The proposed venue for competition should be reflected in training. Surface types, weather conditions and surroundings need to be taken into account.

Illness and Injury

Illness and **injury** affect performance as…

- many injuries are associated with specific sports, which can be caused by the **nature of the game**
- injuries can be caused by **lack of fitness** or readiness for participation.

It should be remembered that…

- being fit **doesn't prevent** the onset of illness
- returning to performance **too quickly** after illness or injury can lead to **poor performance** and further injuries.

Quick Test

1. What does somatotype refer to?
2. What type of person is an ectomorph?
3. What does testosterone do?
4. What can pollution affect?
5. Does fitness prevent the onset of illness?

KEY WORDS
Make sure you understand these words before moving on!
- Mesomorph
- Ectomorph
- Endomorph
- Physique
- Age
- Gender
- Altitude
- Weather differentials

Factors Affecting Performance

Diet and Nutrition

Diet and **nutrition** are important. Athletes need a healthy balanced diet of **seven major components**:

- **Vitamins** and **minerals** in very small amounts.
- **Fats**, **protein** and **carbohydrates** in larger amounts.
- **Fibre** is essential to transport waste material.
- **Water** intake must reflect performance and conditions to prevent **dehydration** and influence temperature control.

Daily intake = Energy expenditure = Stable weight
Daily intake > Energy expenditure = Weight gain
Daily intake < Energy expenditure = Weight loss

Rules for a Healthy Diet
- Carbohydrates – from fruit and vegetables, bread, rice and pasta.
- Protein – low fat sources, e.g. fish, chicken, lean meat, soya.
- Include fat from olive oil and nuts instead of butter and margarine.
- Include foods high in fibre, e.g. fresh fruit and vegetables
- Check nutritional information on food labels.
- Drink lots of water, especially when exercising.

The Healthy Heptagon

Carbohydrates are broken down to glucose to provide fast-release energy.

Protein provides the 'fabric' for the soft tissues; essential for growth and repair.

The body is mostly **water**. You need to replace fluids lost in urine, sweating and breathing.

Fibre / roughage is indigestible plant material that helps to avoid constipation.

Fats contain energy that's stored for slow release.

Vitamin A (milk, butter, fish) for healthy skin, night vision; **Vitamin C** (citrus fruits, vegetables) helps prevent scurvy; **Vitamin D** (milk, fish, eggs, sunshine) prevents rickets.

Minerals – iron (e.g. in liver, green vegetables) prevents thyroid problems; calcium (e.g. in milk, cheese) produces strong bones and teeth.

Special Diets

Different diets suit different sports as food is eaten to produce **energy**.

Athletes vary amounts of fats, carbohydrates and protein, depending on their event.

Foods such as bread, potatoes and rice contain **carbohydrate**. → Carbohydrate is digested to form **glucose**. → Glucose passes through the wall of the stomach into the **blood**. → The blood carries some glucose to the **muscles**. → The glucose is stored in the muscles as **glycogen**. → Glycogen breaks down to glucose when the muscles work to produce **energy**.

Factors Affecting Performance

Special Diets (cont.)

Water is the most **vital component** of a diet. When you exercise you lose water through **sweat**. This needs to be replaced to avoid dehydration. Drink water **before**, **during** and especially **after an** event. Regular, small amounts during the event is best.

High-level endurance sports require a diet **higher** in carbohydrates to provide energy for **long periods**. Endurance athletes may change their diet by carbo-loading before a big event:

1. They **reduce** their body carbohydrate stores by eating a diet of protein and fat for three days, a week before the event.

2. For three days leading up to the event, they eat **lots of carbohydrate** and **train lightly**. This raises carbohydrate stores in the form of **glycogen** in their muscles, so their muscles can **work longer**.

Athletes of **strength events** will often do lots of weight training. They eat more protein to help muscles grow and repair. Protein is broken down into **amino acids**, which are then restructured to form **muscle protein**.

Lifestyle

Training for fitness includes an overall sense of…
- **physical well-being** – a body working well, free from illness and injury
- **mental well-being** – relaxed attitude, stress-free mind and feeling of contentment
- **social well-being** – warm, contented existence in a settled social environment, e.g. friendship and a sense of self-worth in society.

A healthy lifestyle should include work / school, physical exercise and time to relax.

Factors that contribute to a healthy lifestyle are…
- **sleep** – needs to be ample and of good quality
- **attitude** – a positive approach is essential but must include respect for fellow players
- good **personal hygiene** – helps avoid infection and never harms your social life
- **safety** – if your job or hobby could cause injury, take precautions using safety equipment
- **diet** – the correct balance of food types
- **alcohol** / **drug** use – misuse leads to poor health; passive smoking is bad for you too.

Quick Test

1. What are the components of the Healthy Heptagon?
2. Who would include carbo-loading in their diet?
3. What helps muscles grow for strength events?
4. What sort of attitude is needed for a healthy lifestyle?
5. What does freedom from illness and injury contribute to?

KEY WORDS
Make sure you understand these words before moving on!
- Vitamin
- Mineral
- Fat
- Protein
- Carbohydrate
- Dehydration
- Energy
- Carbo-loading

Skill

Skill — OCR

A **skill** is a **physical movement** that is…
- a **learned response** to a **stimulus**
- a **predetermined** movement pattern
- performed with **minimum outlay and effort**.

There are two types of skill:
- **Open** – skills most influenced by external factors.
- **Closed** – skills follow a set pattern of movement, regardless of external factors.

Skills are classified in the following ways:
- **Basic** – skills learned at an early age, such as running, jumping. These form the basis of more complex skills.
- **Complex** – skills specific to a given sport, e.g. the tennis serve. They're made up of a number of basic skills.
- **Internal** paced – you decide when to perform the skill.
- **External** paced – factors outside your control affect when the skill must be performed.

There are two types of skill: OPEN ← → CLOSED

What you do to achieve the same outcome may vary. A goalkeeper's skill is open. He has to stop the ball going into the net. The way he does this depends on how the ball is aimed.

You do the same thing over and over again, in exactly the same way. A golfer's skill is closed.

Guidance — OCR

Guidance is the help received when learning a new skill.

THREE TYPES OF GUIDANCE

VISUAL – WHAT YOU SEE
You learn how to perform a skill by watching first. This may be a one-to-one demonstration or you could watch a video or look at a series of pictures. This could give a clear image in the performer's mind of what's required.

VERBAL – WHAT YOU ARE TOLD
A skill may be explained using words, either by your coach or teacher. The explanation could be used to highlight the most important parts of the visual guidance.

MANUAL – WHAT YOU FEEL
You are physically guided or manhandled through the motions of a new skill in order to learn it. You get a feel for what you should be doing. Your muscles can experience what the movement should feel like. This creates **muscle memory**.

Skill

Learning Skills — OCR

Skills are learned in several ways:

- **Part learning** – the skill is **broken down** into manageable parts. Each part is learned and the parts are put together, e.g. in a tennis serve you learn to throw the ball up, how to grip and swing the racket, and foot position.
- **Whole learning** – **repeating the skill** as one exercise, without breaking it into parts. Dribbling in soccer doesn't lend itself to being split into parts.
- By **fixed practice** – the repeated practice of a closed skill regardless of environmental conditions, e.g. golfers will practise driving this way.
- By **variable practice** – used when practising or learning an open skill, e.g. the way a soccer player kicks the ball depends on the grass, wind and rain.

Feedback — OCR

Information relating to the performance of a skill can be gained through **fast and focused feedback:**

- **Intrinsic feedback** – felt or sensed by the performer from inside the body; the performance feels right or wrong.
- **Extrinsic feedback** – comes from outside the body. It could be a crowd reaction, a coach's comment or the analysis of a video performance.

There are two components of feedback:

- **Knowledge of performance** (**KP**) – knowing how well you performed regardless of the results.
- **Knowledge of results** (**KR**) – tells you what you achieved but not how you did it.

KP and KR give an accurate assessment of how you performed and avoid **'false' outcomes**:

- You performed badly but won because of weak opposition or good luck.
- You performed well but lost because of strong opposition or bad luck.

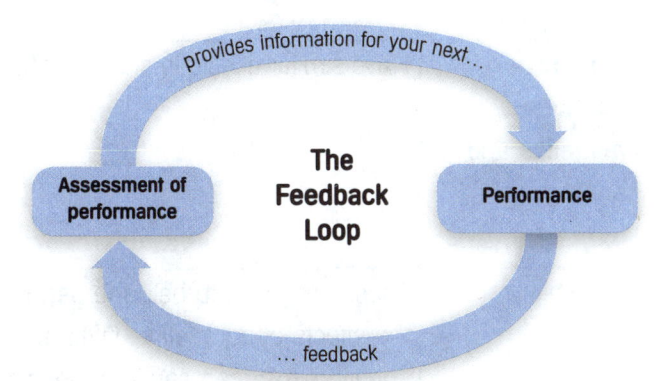

The Feedback Loop: Performance → ...feedback → Assessment of performance → provides information for your next... → Performance

Quick Test

1. What kind of response is skill?
2. What kind of movement is skill?
3. During what age period are basic skills learned?
4. Where does intrinsic feedback come from?
5. Where does extrinsic feedback come from?

KEY WORDS

Make sure you understand these words before moving on!

- Open skill
- Closed skill
- Basic skill
- Complex skill
- Paced skill
- Guidance
- Part learning
- Whole learning
- Knowledge of Performance
- Knowledge of Results

Drugs in Sport

Acceptable Drug Use

Some drugs are acceptable in sport. **Acceptable drug** uses are…
- some **asthmatic** treatments
- some **hayfever** treatments
- some **prescribed drugs** for illness and injury.

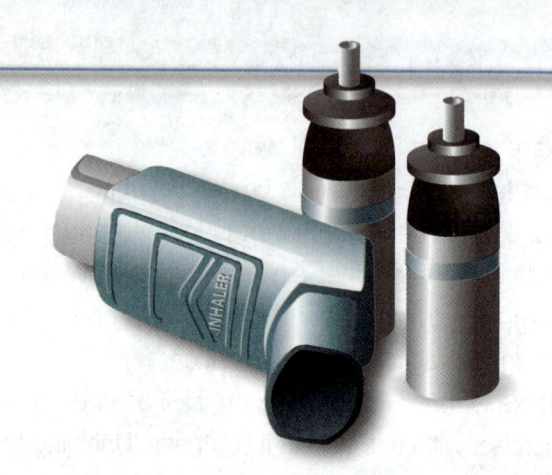

Unacceptable Drug Use

Many drugs are unacceptable in sport.

Drug	Description
Anabolic agents (steroids)	These **accelerate** the **growth and repair** of **muscle** and are often abused to help 'bulk up' for explosive events. This can cause heart and blood pressure problems, excess aggression, male characteristics in females and possible loss of fertility.
Peptide hormones, **mimetics** and **analogues**	Have similar effects to steroids. Many are **artificially produced**.
Beta-blockers	These are taken to help the performer **relax** and counteract the effects of adrenaline. Often useful in archery and shooting, they can cause **abnormal blood pressure**, **insomnia**, and **depression**.
Diuretics	**Remove fluids** by excessive urination to bring about speedy **short-term weight loss**. These are often useful for boxers and wrestlers who have to make a certain weight category. Diuretics cause the loss of soluble vitamins and minerals and can act as **masking agents** for other banned substances.
Narcotic analgesics (painkillers)	These are used to suppress pain from injury and can **increase the pain threshold** during competition. This can lead to the injuries worsening. Examples are heroin, morphine and codeine.

Drugs in Sport

Unacceptable Drug Use (cont)

Drug	Description
Stimulants	**Increase alertness** and **reduce fatigue**. They can increase competitiveness and aggression. They can also cause depression.
Alcohol	Can induce **feelings of well-being** and **lack of responsibility**. It can lead to aggression, reduced glycogen levels, and kidney and liver damage.
Tobacco	A **relaxant** but it **reduces oxygen-carrying capabilities**. It **increases heart rate and blood pressure** and can lead to blocked arteries, excessive coughing, emphysema and possibly cancer.
Blood doping	This is a **forbidden practice** rather than a drug. After training, an athlete removes red cells from their blood, freezes them and re-injects them prior to competition. This gives a **high red cell count** that improves the carrying of oxygen to the muscles, which is necessary for long-distance runners. This can damage the liver and kidneys. The development of **EPO** (erythropoietin) in the 1990s, a drug that artificially stimulates the production of excessive red cells, has similar effects.

Quick Test

1. What are anabolic agents?
2. What do beta-blockers do?
3. What are narcotic analgesics?
4. What reduces fatigue and increases alertness?
5. What is described as a forbidden practice?

KEY WORDS
Make sure you understand these words before moving on!
- Acceptable drug
- Anabolic agent
- Peptide hormone
- Beta-blocker
- Diuretic
- Analgesic
- Stimulant
- EPO

Practice Questions

1) Explain how age affects performance.

_____

_____

2) How does testosterone affect males? Tick the correct options.

    A Makes them bigger ☐

    B Makes them weaker ☐

    C Makes them stop growing ☐

    D Makes them stronger ☐

3) Why do females have a wider pelvis than males?

_____

_____

4) Fill in the missing words to complete the following sentences.

    a) Training at altitude can influence aerobic and anaerobic activities because the air is _____ and oxygen levels are _____.

    b) The seven parts of the Healthy Heptagon are c_____, protein, v_____, fats, fibre, w_____ and minerals.

5) Circle the correct options in the following sentences.

Carbo-loading is when **less / extra / no** carbohydrates are included in the diet for greater energy production in **stamina / sprinting** events.

6) What does protein provide for a weightlifter? Tick the correct options.

    A Muscle growth ☐

    B Muscle repair ☐

    C Muscle reduction ☐

    D Pain relief ☐

7) Give two types of drug that it is acceptable for athletes to use.

    a) _____

    b) _____

Practice Questions

8 Fill in the missing word to complete the following sentence.

Narcotic analgesics enhance performance by suppressing ....

9 What is blood doping? Tick the correct option.

  A Increasing oxygen uptake to improve white cell count ☐

  B Increasing white cell count to improve oxygen uptake ☐

  C Increasing red cell count to improve oxygen uptake ☐

  D Increasing oxygen uptake to improve red cell count ☐

10 Give the three types of well-being that training can induce.

  a) .... b) .... c) ....

11 Give the three aspects of a healthy lifestyle.

  a) .... b) .... c) ....

12 What kind of response is skill? Tick the correct option.

  A Variable ☐

  B Open ☐

  C Fixed ☐

  D Learned ☐

13 Choose the correct words from the options given to complete the sentences below.

  Open   Learned   Variable   Fixed

  a) .... skill is influenced by external factors.

  b) .... practice is when you practise skills in many settings.

14 What are the three types of guidance that can be used when learning a new skill?

  a) .... b) .... c) ....

15 What do the following terms mean?

  a) KP

  ....

  b) KR

  ....

Taking Part

Leisure Time

Leisure time is spare time, i.e. the time not spent at work or school. You have no **commitments** in this time when it is **increasing** in amount.

Leisure time has increased owing to…
- more **labour-saving devices**, e.g. washing machines, microwaves
- quicker travelling times to and from work
- internet home shopping
- a greater range of **convenience foods**
- a **shorter working week**
- people taking **early retirement**
- people having a more flexible or part-time work pattern.

The Amount of Choice in our Daily Lives

- Bodily needs — No choice
- Work
- Work-related activities — Some choice
- Duties and obligations
- Leisure activities — Free choice

Leisure Time Uses

Several factors affect how we spend leisure time:
- **Age** – as people get older they participate in **fewer** activities. Age brings **disabilities** that can affect **participation**.
- **Activities learned at school** can direct you towards sports you know and enjoy.
- **Media and role models** encourage you to take part rather than just watch.
- **Where you live** can influence the activities you do, e.g. coastal and river regions offer boating, the countryside offers outdoor pursuits, i.e. walking, climbing.
- **Campaigns** run by central or local government encourage us to maintain a healthy lifestyle.

Reasons to Take Part

People elect to play sport because…
- it's **enjoyable** and helps them look and feel good
- it can give a **sense of achievement**
- it contributes to **good health** and **aids recovery** from illness
- it **relieves stress** and tensions built up in other parts of their lives
- it's a **social activity** that develops friendships and fosters team involvement
- it can satisfy the **competitive element** in them.

Taking Part

Influences on Taking Part

Group pressures and **personal circumstances** influence our choice of sporting activities:

- **Family** provide an early introduction to activities, together with encouragement and support.
- **Peers** or friends of a similar age and inclination may take part in the same.
- Your **gender** leads you to follow what others do. More males participate in sports activities than females.
- **Race**, **tradition** and **cultural** background often dictate whether to take part in sport. Some cultures discourage female participation.
- The **popularity** of an activity may influence specific participation.
- The **socio-economic situation** of the group influences participation levels. **Unemployment** can limit involvement as some sports are expensive to follow.

Group pressures can exert...	
Positive Factors	Negative Factors
Active	Non-active
Supportive	Alternative interests
Encouraging	Expectations too high
High profile	Too masculine / feminine
Role models	Cultural differences

Quick Test

1. What is your spare time known as?
2. How do governments encourage you to lead a healthy lifestyle?
3. How does where you live influence your choice of activities?
4. What does playing sport give us a sense of?
5. What are your friends also known as?

KEY WORDS
Make sure you understand these words before moving on!
- Labour-saving device
- Commitments
- Convenience food
- Shorter working week
- Participation
- Media and role models
- Race
- Tradition
- Culture

Participation

Participation Factors

Participation in sporting activities is affected by a number of factors:

- **Age** – some sports lend themselves to certain age groups. The biggest post-school participation levels are around the ages of 18–20 and 35–40.
- **Attitude** – set by our parents, peer groups and role models. If they play, then we tend to. If they played, then they tend to encourage us to play.
- **Access** – **proximity** and **ease of access** are important, as are opening times and whether both major and minority interests are catered for.
- **Climate** / **environment** – top winter sports performers come from cold mountainous regions. Winter sports facilities aren't always available locally in summer and vice versa.
- **Fashion** – some sports are trendy to do, but trends change. Keep-fit and related aerobic activities are popular today.
- **Finance** – money is often a ruling factor. **Concession rates** for certain age groups may exist and providers might subsidise some activities.
- **Schools** – what is learned at school can establish **lifelong habits**.

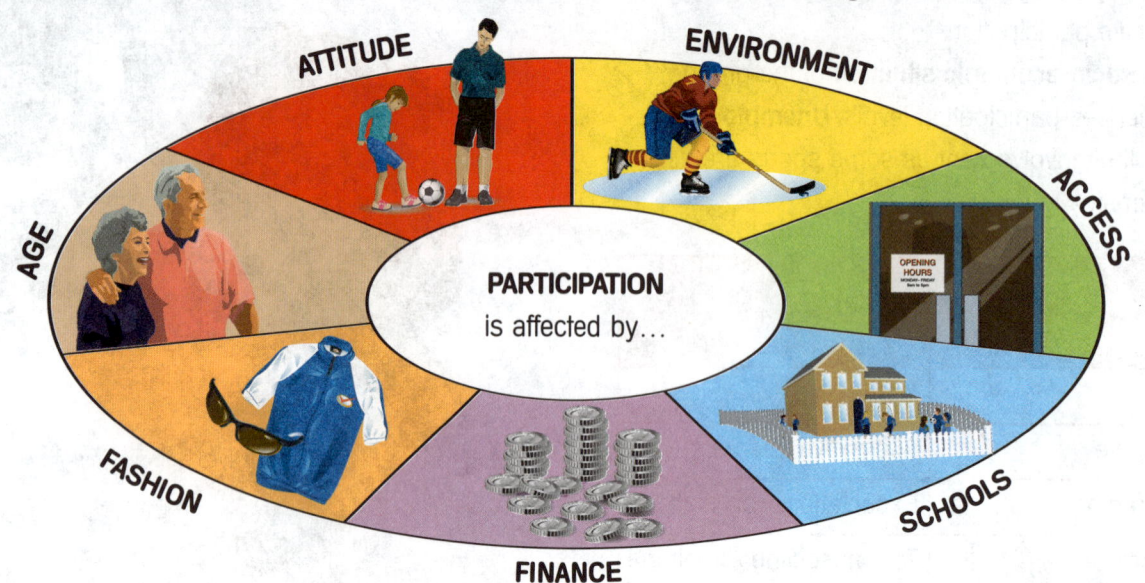

Health and Hygiene

There are many personal health and hygiene aspects to consider:

- **Clothing** should be clean and appropriate to the activity. Clean clothes **smell better** and help **prevent bacteria spreading**.
- **Feet** should be checked for **athlete's foot** (a fungal growth between and around the toes), and **verrucas** (warts under the feet caused by a viral infection).
- Shoes should fit well. If they're too tight or loose they can cause corns, blisters and bunions.
- **Sweating** produces an excellent breeding ground for bacteria. Deodorants hide the smell but only a shower can remove the bacteria.
- **Teeth** should be kept clean and may need gum shields or mouth protectors in some sports.
- **Nails** should be kept clean and short to prevent the accidental scratching of opponents. Long hair should be tied back so that it can't be pulled accidentally.
- **Tissues** and **handkerchiefs** should be used correctly and where appropriate.
- **Vaccinations** should be used to help stop the spread of diseases – prevention is better than cure.

Participation

Foot Health and Hygiene

There are two 'classic' foot infections.

Athlete's foot…
- is a **fungal growth** between the toes
- is found in warm and moist places
- causes the skin to crack and peel, making it itchy.

To treat athlete's foot…
- keep feet **clean** and **dry**
- dry between toes after showering
- use **athlete's foot cream**, **spray** or **talc**.

Verrucas…
- are **warts** on the feet and are **easily spread**
- are **hard to get rid** of and can be **painful**
- are caused by a **virus**.

To treat verrucas…
- use a **verruca sock** to prevent others becoming infected
- apply **ointment** to the affected area
- see a doctor or chiropodist in severe cases, who will freeze dry the verucca off your foot.

Avoid verrucas by using flip-flops in communal areas.

Tight Shoes

Tight shoes can cause three 'classic' problems:

1. **Corns** – **callouses** of thick horny skin that form on joints of toes or balls of feet, where the foot has pressed hard against the shoe.
2. **Bunions** – form at the joint between the big toe and the foot when the joint capsule becomes inflamed, as a result of **pressure from tight shoes**.
3. **Blisters** – caused by the foot rubbing against the shoe, a particular problem with new shoes. You should break new shoes in **gradually**.

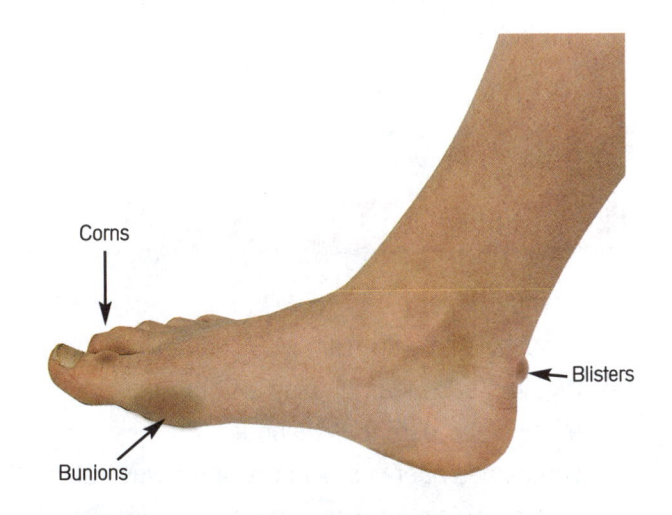

Quick Test

1. Who, besides parents and role models, help to set our attitudes to participation?
2. Who is likely to get a concession rate?
3. What can appear as warts under the feet?
4. How should teeth be protected in a game?
5. What is prevention better than?

KEY WORDS

Make sure you understand these words before moving on!
- Age
- Attitude
- Access
- Environment
- Fashion
- Finance
- Athlete's foot
- Sweating
- Vaccinations

The Way to Play

Competitions

There are three main systems of competition:
- **Ladder** system
- **League** system
- **Knockout** system.

The Ladder System

The ladder system…
- is usually employed in **individual sports**, e.g. tennis, badminton, squash
- allows **individuals** to play competitively with players of a similar standard
- allows **one player to challenge another**, who is a limited number of places above them – a successful challenge results in **promotion** up the ladder.

LEADERBOARD

1. A Player
2. S O Else
3. M R Taylor
4. A Chance
5. B A Newman

The League System

The league system…
- is associated with **team play**
- requires each team to play a fixture against every other team in the league
- sometimes operates a '**home and away**' rule
- awards points for wins, draws and sometimes losses. Teams level on points are separated by goal difference.

Pos	Team	P	W	D	L	F	A	PTS
1	Sandbach	9	7	2	0	16	5	23
2	Middlewich	9	7	1	1	12	7	22
3	Kidsgrove	9	6	2	1	13	5	20
4	Biddulph	9	5	2	2	11	7	17
5	Sale	9	5	1	3	9	4	16

The Knockout System

The knockout system…
- can be used for **individual** or **team** competitions
- usually involves a **draw** to find out an opponent; future opponents are met in the next round
- sometimes uses **seeding** to try to get the better teams to meet in the later stages.

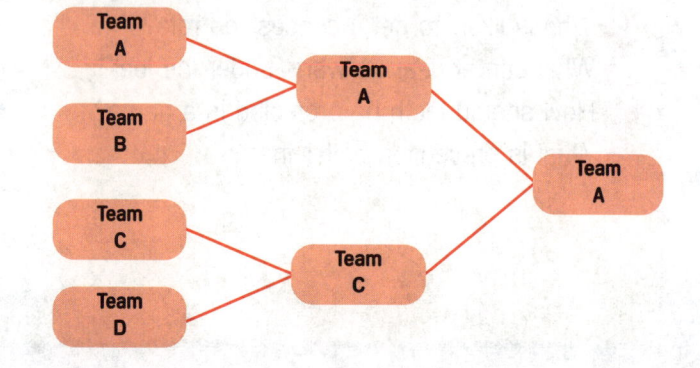

The Way to Play

Sporting Behaviour

Sporting behaviour is dictated by the way you play. Players must **obey the rules**…
- to assist in the **organisation** and running of the game
- to ensure the **safety** of all concerned
- to add to the **enjoyment** of playing the game.

Rules are established by national organisations but may be adapted to suit local needs. Players must know the rules thoroughly in order to play fairly.

Rule enforcement…
- must be **effective**
- can mean being **penalised** by a loss of points, free kicks, or similar if you fail to follow the rules
- is essential and serious rule breaches may result in **punishment** (i.e. sin bins, suspensions, expulsions, bans and fines)
- must be carried out to ensure both the **safety** of players and fair play.

Sports Etiquette

Sports etiquette isn't a rule but it is expected during play. It's often referred to as an unwritten rule that…
- is a conventional form of behaviour
- **reflects fair play** and good sporting attitudes
- is generally accepted as the '**way to play**'.

Fair play is often referred to as the **spirit of sportsmanship** but is often overlooked when a professional '**win at all costs**' attitude is adopted.

Quick Test

1. What type of sport suits a ladder system of competition?
2. What is it called when a knockout system arranges for teams to meet later in the competition?
3. Who must a team play in a league system?
4. Who establishes the rules of a sport?
5. What is known as the unwritten rule of sport?

KEY WORDS
Make sure you understand these words before moving on!
- Ladder
- League
- Knockout
- Seeding
- Rule enforcement
- Spirit of sportsmanship

Modern Technology

Equipment Advances

Technological developments have had a big impact on the equipment used in sport.

Developments related to **equipment**:
- **Starting guns** connected to **timing devices** allow for the recording of speed and **more accurate starts** in a sprint race.
- **Sensors** record the position of marathon runners. Sensors are also used in body suits to register a hit in fencing.
- **Computerised trigonometry** enables the measuring of distances thrown to be more accurate.
- The use of **man-made materials** (e.g. graphite, carbon fibre) in tennis rackets, golf clubs and poles (allowing performers to hit harder, stronger and jump higher).
- Improved rubber and foam **landing mats** in athletics and gymnastics allow performers to land badly without injury. The Fosbury Flop couldn't be performed without these.

Camera Technology

Developments related to **digital images**:
- **Cameras** show if a tennis ball is in or out, or if a cricketer is run out.
- Cameras provide **instant feedback** to help decision making, e.g. the finish of a 100-metre event, when photographs show the finishing order and times.
- **Large screens** provide spectators with a better view of events and instantly show results.

ICT in Sport

Aspects of **information and computer technology** (**ICT**) are successfully applied to sport.

Monitors are readily available for most athletes. Some can be attached to the chest to monitor heart rate whilst others are attached to equipment to measure power.

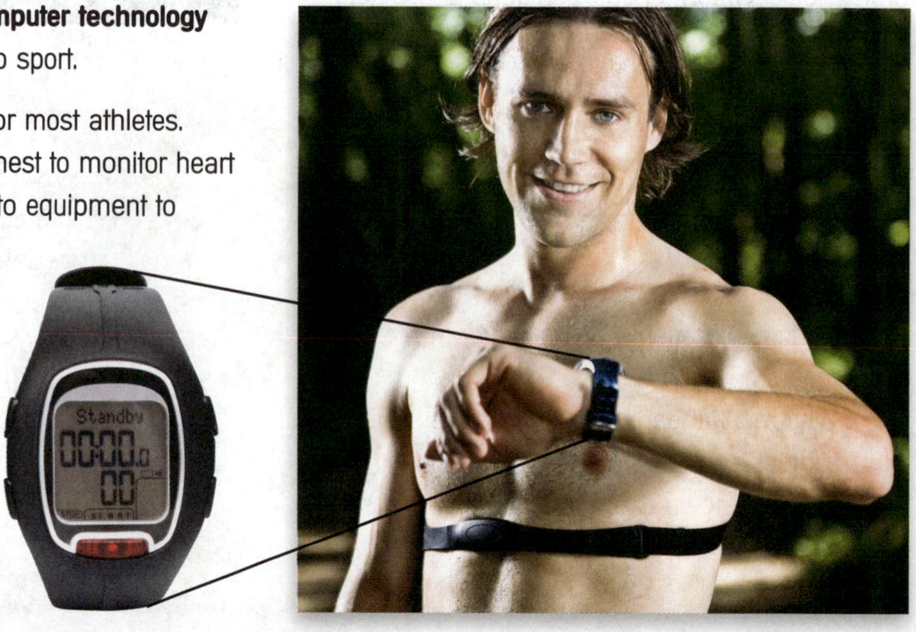

Modern Technology

ICT in Sport (cont.)

Computer programs are used to **track the performance** of individual players and teams, helping to **identify their strengths and weaknesses**. Programs have been developed to **assist officials** in **decision making** in cricket and tennis.

Visual analysis is the **use of playbacks** to establish an analysis of **movement patterns**. This helps individuals to **refine skill performance**.

Back Somersault

Multimedia in Sport

DVDs and **CD-ROMs** provide information or instruction on a wide range of sporting activity. **Websites** are the information providers for sports, be it for teams, clubs or individuals.

In addition, **interactive sites** show examples of skill, performance, training and testing.

Quick Test

1. What type of material is graphite?
2. What special type of landing area is needed for the Fosbury Flop?
3. What does visual analysis help to refine?
4. How are computer programs helpful when tracking an athlete's performance?
5. How can sensors be useful in a marathon?

KEY WORDS
Make sure you understand these words before moving on!
- Man-made material
- Instant feedback
- Monitors
- Website

Training Aids

Training Aids

An athlete's **clothing** can affect performance. **Body suits** are worn to **reduce drag** and **increase speed**. Full suits were first seen with cyclists and speed skaters, later becoming accepted for athletes and swimmers. Many players wear adapted suits to **keep warm** or **protect** from the impact of a collision.

Safety equipment is now made of **stronger** but **lighter** materials. Shin pads, head guards and cricket pads now offer more protection and don't hinder movement. Hockey goalkeepers have bigger, lighter **protective clothing** and equipment.

Clothing **constantly changes** as new materials evolve. Clothing is expected to insulate, but should also work in extreme heat. **Nylon** is a good heat-retaining material whilst **neoprene** keeps a body warm in water. The design of the running vest allows for the **effective dispersion of body heat** while running.

Footwear

Each sport requires participants to wear **specialist footwear.**

Track runners wear **spikes**. Road runners wear footwear with **rubber soles**.	Rugby players and footballers wear **boots** with **studs**.	Cricketers wear footwear with **spikes** or **rubber soles**.	Golfers wear footwear with **spikes** or **rubber soles**.

Playing Safe

Safety Considerations

All practical activities involve **hazardous situations**. It's important to try to **minimise risk**. You should…

- check all equipment is **working**
- complete the appropriate **warm-up**
- check the **playing surface** is safe (i.e. no dust or broken glass)
- **dress appropriately** and follow all instructions
- always use the **correct playing technique** and follow the rules
- always **consult the person in charge** if in doubt about a safety issue.

Organisers should carry out a **risk assessment** before starting work. Each activity requires that certain aspects be considered.

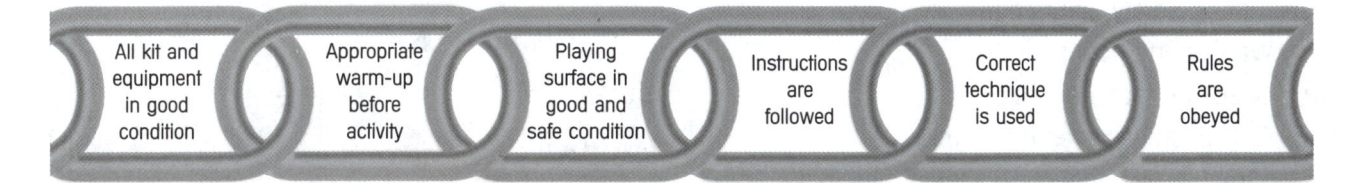

| All kit and equipment in good condition | Appropriate warm-up before activity | Playing surface in good and safe condition | Instructions are followed | Correct technique is used | Rules are obeyed |

Consider the Activity

Safety aspects to be considered in gymnastics, trampoline and dance:

- The **condition** of mats and floors (wet or dusty floors cause slipping).
- The presence of **qualified supervision** and the use of **spotters**.
- The provision of **sufficient headspace**.
- The observance of the **no jewellery rule**, wearing appropriate clothing and the use of hand guards and soft chalk (magnesium carbonate).
- The **use of help** and the **correct method** when lifting equipment.

Games activities require that…

- the surface is **clear of obstructions and debris**
- the surroundings provide a **safe area**
- **individual protective equipment** (gum shields, face masks, shin pads) is available
- **group equipment** (batting pads, padded gloves) is available and in good condition
- posts are protected
- nets are properly secured.

Quick Test

1. What can cause slipping on a playing surface?
2. What is the proper name for the chalk used in gymnastics?
3. What are gum shields, face masks and shin pads examples of?
4. What helps to reduce drag for swimmers?
5. What type of material keeps the body warm in water?

KEY WORDS
Make sure you understand these words before moving on!
- Safety equipment
- Protective clothing
- Playing surface
- Spotter

Playing Safe

Athletics Safety

Athletic activities require that…
- **running areas** are clear of obstructions and debris
- **landing areas** are clear, with sand well raked and rakes kept out of pits
- **throwing areas** are well marked out and caged
- **warning sounds** are used to indicate that throws are taking place
- **no running** to collect javelins is allowed
- waiting participants stay behind the throwers.

Swimming Safety

Swimming safety instructions:
- Walk on the pool side.
- Check for the deep end.
- Only use boards as directed.
- Jump or dive only under supervision in the designated area.
- Use only approved artificial aids.

Outdoor Safety

Outdoor pursuits require you to…
- check the weather
- check personal equipment
- **check safety equipment** including emergency first aid, and take emergency rations as appropriate
- **plan a detailed route** on paper and list your escape routes; leave a copy with someone so they know where you're going and when you're due back.

During outdoor pursuits…
- remember that **fatigue can cause injuries**
- follow the **NGB rules**
- be aware of potential risk and **don't take unnecessary risks**
- be responsible for your own safety as well as others'
- follow any instructions given.

Lifting and Carrying

Lifting — AQA

Injuries occur while you're preparing for an activity and can sometimes be quite serious.

Use the **correct technique** when lifting equipment and…
- always **bend the knees**
- keep the **arms bent**
- keep the load **close to the body**
- keep a **straight back**
- lift using the leg muscles
- keep your **head up**
- don't lift above the head without assistance.

When lowering equipment, the opposite procedure should be followed with an emphasis on a **straight back**.

Carrying — AQA

When carrying equipment, remember…
- that javelins must be carried **vertically**
- that large objects will need at least two people
- that multiple carriers must **work together**, not pull or push each other
- to look where you're going.

Always remember that you should lift, carry and work within your own capabilities.

Quick Test

1. What is the correct way to move along a pool side?
2. When would you plan an escape route?
3. How should you carry javelins?
4. Should your back be bent or straight when lifting?
5. During outdoor pursuits, what can fatigue lead to?

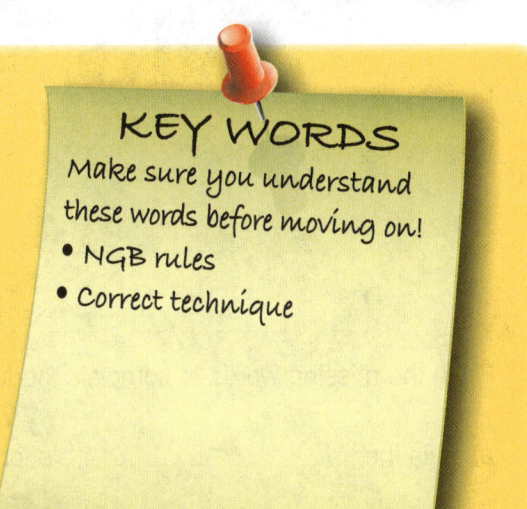

KEY WORDS
Make sure you understand these words before moving on!
- NGB rules
- Correct technique

Practice Questions

1 What is leisure time?

....

2 What influence have labour-saving goods had on leisure time? Tick the correct option.

    A Increased the amount of leisure time ☐

    B Reduced the amount of leisure time ☐

    C Left no time for leisure ☐

3 What are peers?

....

4 Explain how age affects participation.

....

....

....

5 Fill in the missing words to complete the following sentences.

Sweating is a breeding ground for .... These can be removed by ....

6 What are the three main formats of competition?

    a) ....

    b) ....

    c) ....

7 What is 'seeding'?

....

....

8 Fill in the missing words to complete the following sentences.

    a) It is the ....'s job to enforce the rules.

    b) Another term for fair play is spirit of ....

Practice Questions

9 What modern technology do officials use to check on the position of marathon runners? Tick the correct option.

    A Pedometers ☐   **B** Microphones ☐

    C Sensors ☐   **D** Body suits ☐

10 What are the most common monitors used in sport?

_____

11 Circle the correct option in the following sentence.

Other than keeping warm, the purpose of a body suit is to **increase** / **reduce** drag.

12 Which performers are most likely to wear body suits? Give three examples.

a) _____

b) _____

c) _____

13 Is the following statement **true** or **false**?

The materials nylon and neoprene don't help to retain body heat. _____

14 Fill in the missing words to complete the following sentences.

a) Organisers of sporting activities should carry out a _____ assessment before any performance takes place.

b) Jumping and diving in swimming pools should take place in a _____ area with the use of approved _____ .

15 Choose the correct words from the options given to complete the sentences below.

    up   **down**   **arms**   **leg**

    straight   **bent**

When lifting an object, you should keep the head _____ , the _____ bent and the back _____ . The _____ muscles should mostly be used.

Sponsorship

Sponsorship

Sponsorship is a **commercial transaction** - the sport or performer acts as an advertising site for products in return for **financial or material support**.

Sponsorship works by…
- a **company** or **business giving support**
- a **sporting body**, **team** or **individual** getting **support**
- promoting a **company name** or **logo**.

If the sport or performer is successful…
- the company image is improved
- a **boost in sales** takes place
- the performer or sport will get **more sponsorship**.

Forms of Sponsorship

Sponsorship takes many forms, including the provision of…
- **equipment** such as balls, rackets, even sailing boats and skis
- **clothing** – all the performer's sportswear
- accessories, such as watches and sunglasses, not essential to the sport but still promoting a company
- **transport** and **travel** – this could include a free car, reduced travel costs or even assistance with moving equipment
- **training costs** – the cost of hiring facilities, specialist coaches or even warm weather training
- **money** – a full-time athlete can't earn a wage so a company might pay daily living expenses in return for public appearances or for advertising a product.

Sponsorship can be given to…
- a **sport**, e.g. Amateur Swimming Association
- a **team**, e.g. Premiership football teams
- **events**, e.g. World Snooker Championship
- **competitions** e.g. the Super League (Rugby League)
- **individuals**, e.g. personal contracts with sportswear companies.

Sponsorship

Obtaining Sponsorship

Some sports attract more sponsorship than others. It's **harder** for **minority sports** to attract big-money sponsors.

Easier to attract sponsorship: Football, Formula 1, City marathons, Members of national teams

Harder to attract sponsorship: Netball, Hockey, Volleyball, Badminton

Advantages of Sponsorship
Aids potential young stars' development.
Reduces financial pressures, enabling full-time training / competing.
Funds events by covering organisational and administrative costs.
Provision of coaching, equipment, travel and specialist facilities.
An increased income, resulting in superstar salary status.

Disadvantages of Sponsorship
Exploitation to suit the sponsor's needs.
Length of contract may be short, which provides less security.
Support may be withdrawn if the sponsor's income becomes reduced.
Minority sports may decline as major sports attract most sponsorship.
Presents the wrong image through tobacco or alcohol sponsorship.

Quick Test

1. What type of transaction is sponsorship?
2. What, besides money, can be included in sponsorship?
3. What does a company want out of sponsorship of a sport?
4. What types of sport find it difficult to get sponsorship?

KEY WORDS
Make sure you understand these words before moving on!
- Sponsorship
- Assistance
- Exploitation
- Image

Media

Types of Media

Media in sport is the written and electronic coverage of sport.

Media	Audience	Type of Coverage
Internet		Fast information access. Possibly educational and / or entertaining.
Video / film		Recorded entertainment (best action). Educational (coaching series).
Books		Stories behind events. Biographies – for leisure or education.
Magazines		Specialised or general – informative and educational.
Radio		Informative and entertaining with results, reports, comments, etc.
Newspapers (tabloid and broadsheet)		Informative – results, reports, balanced views, opinions, etc. Entertaining – sensational stories, private lives exposed. Educational – tips to develop skills and fitness.
Television (Terrestrial – licence fee. Satellite, cable, digital, interactive – all subscription or pay-per-view)		Informative – results, reports, comment, text, live action, highlights. Entertaining – live action, highlights, specialised programmes. Educational – documentaries, coaching series, live action, highlights, specific programmes for schools.

Effects of the Media

The **media** has made a big impact on our lives over the last 50 years. It likes to **sensationalise** and keeps us **informed** and **entertained**.

The media's **good effects** are that it…
- promotes and popularises sport
- **generates finance** through sponsorship and advertising
- informs, enlightens and instructs
- **develops technical innovations** to give better coverage
- **raises awareness** and interest, which encourages greater participation
- **creates star performers** (good **role models**)
- increases worldwide audiences.

The media's **bad effects** are that it…
- can push minority sports into **decline**
- **increases pressure** on players and coaches
- can create boredom by **overexposure**
- **sensationalises** bad aspects of the sport
- **forces change** on sports rules and schedules to suit TV and sponsors.

The **ugly aspects** of media coverage are that it…
- publicises the poor behaviour of some players and spectators
- creates a 'win at all costs' approach, which encourages cheating
- intensifies the loyalties and rivalries of fans, which can lead to social disorder and riots.

Media

Media and Sponsorship

The media and sponsorship are closely linked. The media is **big business** and wants to make **profit** and wants sponsorship, which is a form of advertising.

Sports audience attracts… Media attention, advertising, sponsorship which results in… Money generated for sport / which results in… Money generated for the media, advertisers and sponsors

Media and Conflict

The media is often in **conflict** with sports. The media…

- wants **maximum event exposure**
- can **influence** the date and time of events
- can **demand** personal appearances
- can insist which sponsorship logos are worn in interviews
- can **undermine officials** – instant replays can change official decisions
- can influence a sport's popularity – no coverage leads to reduced sponsorship, which in turn leads to a sport's decline
- can intrude on a **performer's personal life**
- may reduce attendance at a televised event – potential spectators may stay away if another event is televised
- is denied advertising products such as tobacco, alcohol and some fast foods – these are unsuitable and could give young spectators the wrong message.

Not all sports are affected – events such as the **FA Cup Final** and **Wimbledon** are restricted to the BBC. Although this means they're **free to view**, the restriction could affect the sport's income.

Quick Test

1. Which part of the media draws the largest audience?
2. What does the media generate?
3. What can happen to a sport that gets little or no media coverage?
4. What effect can the media have on match officials?
5. Which sports events are restricted to certain parts of the media?

KEY WORDS
Make sure you understand these words before moving on!
- Media
- Sensationalism
- Entertainment
- Role model
- Overexposure

Politics

Political Interference

National governments have attempted to **influence sports events** on several occasions. The most well-known instances relate to the Olympic Games.

Olympic Games	Interference
1936, Berlin, Germany	Hitler used the Games to further the Nazi cause. He **refused** to acknowledge the success of black US athlete **Jesse Owens**.
1956, Melbourne, Australia	**Spain** and **Holland** withdrew over the Russian invasion of Hungary. **Communist China** withdrew rather than compete against Taiwan.
1964, Tokyo, Japan	**South Africa's** invitation was withdrawn at the last minute because of apartheid.
1968, Mexico City, Mexico	**Black US athletes** drew attention to poor civil rights back home with a **Black Power salute**. **South Africa** was refused admittance due to its political policies.
1972, Munich, Germany	**Rhodesia** was excluded after complaints about its treatment of black citizens. **Arab nationalists** took some of the Israeli team hostage, killing several. The hostage-takers were allowed to escape.
1976, Montreal, Canada	**South Africa** was still excluded. There was a **boycott** by many black African nations over the **New Zealand rugby tour** of South Africa.
1980, Moscow, Russia	The **USA** led a boycott by some western nations in protest over the **USSR** invasion of Afghanistan. Some UK athletes ignored the ban; others supported it.
1984, Los Angeles, USA	The USSR and some Eastern bloc countries boycotted the Games in retaliation for the USA actions in 1980. **Sponsorship** and **TV rights** funded the Games, which meant that the media influenced event times. Some athletes received payments for their success (amateur status having been dropped in 1981).

1970 saw the **expulsion** of South Africa from the Commonwealth and Olympic movements because of its **political ideals**.

1977 saw the signing of the **Gleneagles Agreement** by Commonwealth countries. This reinforced the ban on South Africa, but extended it to include all sporting contact. Only when apartheid was abolished was South Africa allowed back.

Politics

Political Influence

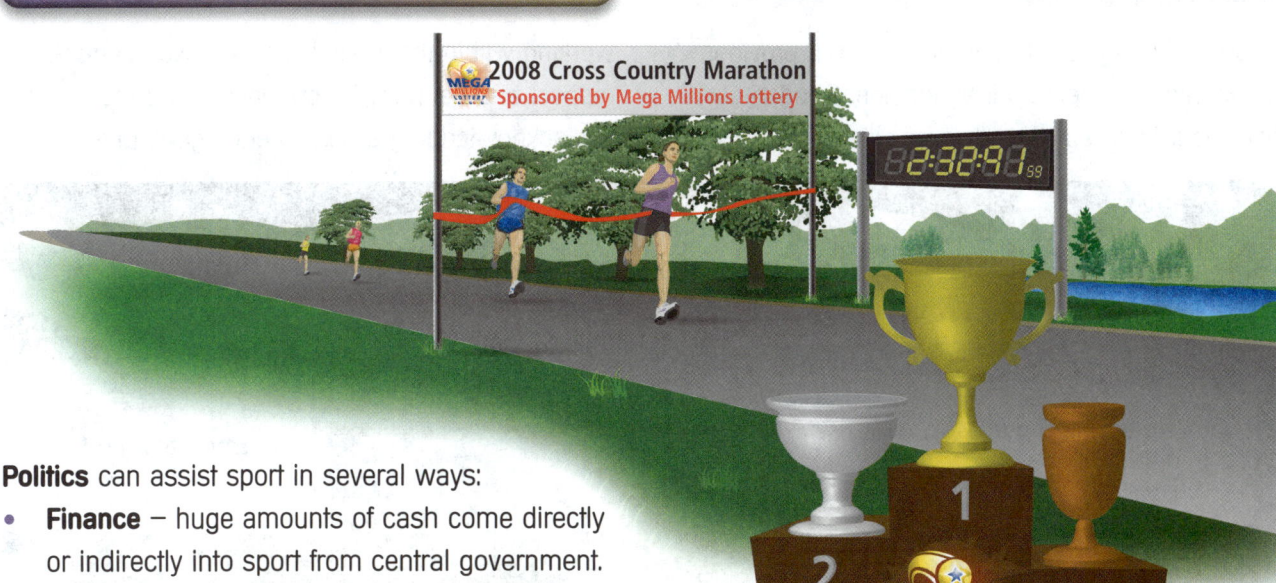

Politics can assist sport in several ways:
- **Finance** – huge amounts of cash come directly or indirectly into sport from central government.
- Establishing a **National Lottery**, which includes sport as a good cause and worthy of special financial support.
- **Organisation** – a **central government** Sports Minister promotes the country's involvement in international sport and sets up a basic local sports structure.
- **Provision** – **Acts of Parliament** relating to sport have been passed, including the compulsory provision of sport in schools and the **National Curriculum**.
- **Legislation** – laws control the safety standards of sporting venues and the care of young performers.
- **Research** – youth sector involvement in sport and sporting disasters such as Hillsborough have been investigated.
- **Specific aid** – governments support individual sports or organisations, such as the **BOA**, to stage international competitions (the most well-known being the 2012 London Olympics).
- The **protection** of some events from commercial TV ensures that sports such as Wimbledon and the FA Cup Final can be seen on 'free to view' television by anyone.
- The development of **health-related programmes**, such as those aimed to combat obesity.

Quick Test

1. Which politician has responsibility for sport in central government?
2. What provides some funding for sport and considers it to be a good cause?
3. Why did Spain and Holland withdraw from the 1956 Games?
4. Which team was sent home from the 1972 Games?
5. When was the Gleneagles Agreement signed?

KEY WORDS
Make sure you understand these words before moving on!
- Gleneagles Agreement
- Central Government
- Acts of Parliament
- Legislation

Sporting Behaviour

Good Behaviour

Sport can bring about **good behaviour**. It provides an emotional outlet to relieve tension. Good behaviour involves controlling **aggression** and working within the rules. It also involves **etiquette**, respect and courtesy for opponents and the game, e.g. acknowledging an opponent's good play.

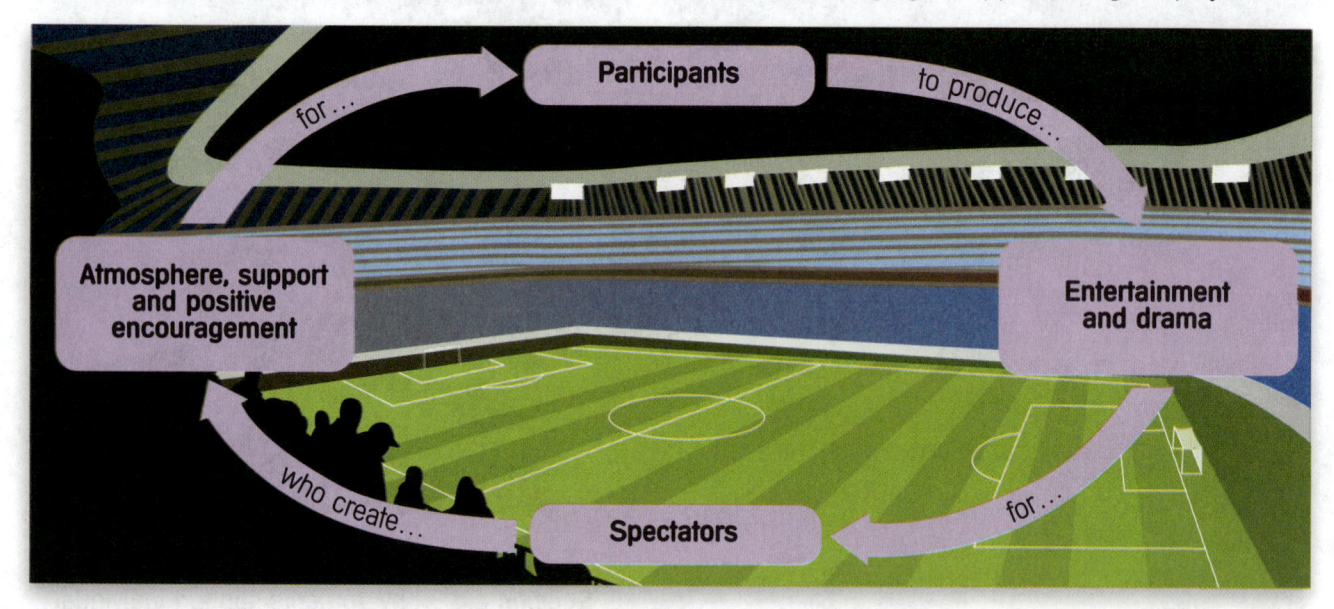

Bad Behaviour

Sport can influence the adoption of **anti-social behaviour**. Participation can lead to…
- **over-aggression** – foul play, deliberate fouls (**professional fouls**)
- **gamesmanship**, e.g. diving, timewasting
- **cheating**, using unfair tactics
- attempts to disrupt the opposition by **sledging** (unfairly psyching-out opponents)
- **intimidating officials** by challenging decisions, leading to self-doubt by officials who then don't act firmly
- **adverse spectator behaviour**, e.g. swearing, abuse, fighting.

Spectators

Spectators can have **good points**:
- They can influence a match; cheering a team on can **lift players**, so playing at home can be an advantage.
- They buy tickets, which contributes to the club's income; in some team sports the clubs divide the match income between the home and away sides.
- They buy club merchandise, such as shirts and scarves.
- They often buy **social membership** to a club, which helps its finances.

Sporting Behaviour

Spectators (cont.)

Spectators can have **bad points**:
- They can **influence** when a game is played.
- They can **intimidate visiting players** in an attempt to put them off.
- They need **extra facilities** to watch the game from, such as a stadium, sometimes with a seating area.
- They require marshals to **supervise crowds**.
- They might require the home club to pay for **extra police**.
- They may not be true supporters, but more interested in **hooliganism**.
- They may carry bad behaviour into the surrounding streets.
- They may bring the game and sport into **disrepute**, forcing away genuine fans.

Football Hooliganism

Football hooliganism fully developed in the 1970s and 1980s and is…
- sometimes fuelled by events on the pitch, but more often by **drunkenness**
- bad behaviour that some attempt to excuse on the grounds of **loyalty** to a team, region or country
- violence that can take place at matches as well as outside the stadium in host cities.

Tragedies at **Heysel** in 1985 and **Hillsborough** in 1989 led to a **Government enquiry** to establish the causes of hooliganism, how to combat crowd violence and how to prevent future tragedies. It produced the **Taylor Report**, which made important recommendations.

THE TAYLOR REPORT

Recommendations and other measures included:
- Removal of perimeter fences.
- All-seater stadiums.
- Fan segregation.
- CCTV.
- Police forces sharing intelligence about troublemakers.

Quick Test

1. What does good sporting behaviour relieve?
2. What is sporting etiquette?
3. What is football hooliganism?
4. When did football hooliganism become evident?
5. Name the report related to football hooliganism.

KEY WORDS
Make sure you understand these words before moving on!
- Aggression
- Gamesmanship
- Sledging
- Adverse spectator behaviour

Sporting Status

Playing for Pay

Most people participate in sport for **enjoyment** alone. Others want to supplement this enjoyment, which has led to categories of players:
- **Amateurs** take part for enjoyment **without pay**.
- **Professionals** get paid for taking part – for them sport is a **full-time job**.
- **Semi-professionals** have a regular job but are paid to play **part-time**.
- **Shamateurs** are players who claim to be amateurs but do in fact get paid.

Status

Players are only eligible to take part in **certain competitions**:
- **Open competitions** are for **all** (amateurs and professionals). Amateurs aren't allowed to keep any prize money, although some are allowed to take goods as prizes.
- **Amateur competitions** are only open to **genuine amateurs**, not professionals, semi-professionals or shamateurs.

Standards vary but as more and more sports become open, the standard steadily rises.

It was in 1968 that the famous Wimbledon tennis tournament became the first grand slam event to become open.

Changes to Status

Over the last 30 years players' financial rewards have changed. In the recent past…
- rules relating to payments were often 'bent' by players and officials
- players received payments but claimed to be amateur so they could compete in amateur events like the Olympics
- **trust funds** were established – players' payments were paid into a fund that was drawn on for expenses, the remainder to be used on retiring
- some players were given **dubious employment** – they might join the army but be allowed to train and compete full-time
- some colleges and universities, especially those in the USA, offered sports scholarships so students could train and compete full-time
- **training expenses** would be paid, providing the athlete competed when required
- some competitions gave valuable **gift payments** to winners and other competitors, such as cars that could be traded in at a later date
- **illegal payments** (**boot money**) were common in rugby – players came off the field to find cash in their shoes.

Sporting Status

Changes to Sports

Most sports now **embrace payments**:
- Most sports have removed the distinction between amateur and professional.
- Although professional football was established in 1884, amateurs and professionals now **mix** in competitions.
- Although 1895 saw rugby split into two codes (one amateur, the other professional), in 1995 rugby union became professional with amateurs playing alongside professionals.
- Most professional sports are for men; those for women are lagging a long way behind.

A Few Professionals
Full-time players, expected to reach the highest standards.

Some Semi-Professionals
Part-time players, committed to their sport, performing at a very good level.

Many Amateurs
Spare-time players who provide most sport participants. It's possible for players to keep amateur status and continue their sport full-time through…
- **scholarships** for athletes at specialist colleges
- trust funds – use prize/appearance money to pay expenses
- sponsorship by a private enterprise
- grants from Sports Aid
- their occupation – generous employer allowing time off to train / compete.

These may be seen as 'loopholes', allowing amateurs to earn from their sport.

Quick Test

1. What do amateurs not get for playing sports?
2. What do most semi-professionals have that a professional might not have?
3. Who can take part in an open competition?
4. What was trust fund money used for?
5. What do most sports now embrace?

KEY WORDS
Make sure you understand these words before moving on!
- Amateur
- Professional
- Semi-professional
- Shamateur
- Open competition
- Amateur competition
- Gift payment
- Boot money
- Scholarship

Discrimination

Women in Sport

Few women played sport in the **1800s**. It was considered…
- that physical activity was for **men only**
- that lower-class women had no time or money for sport
- **unattractive** and **unladylike** for women to race about in a sporting manner
- that strenuous competition was **inappropriate** for women
- that women might harm themselves and their clothing was unsuitable
- that women should look after the home and **rear children**
- that only gentle riding, walking, badminton and tennis were acceptable.

Changing Times

Sports were organised and controlled **by men for men**. In the 1900s attitudes began to change because…
- womens' clothing became **more suitable for sport**; the corset went out of fashion and the brassiere was invented
- girls began to be taught sport in schools
- more women worked and had time and money to spend on sport
- **class distinction** was **changing** and sport was considered a **healthy, social pastime for all**
- **motherhood** was no longer seen as a barrier – at the 1948 Olympics, Fanny Blankers-Koen, a mother of two, won four gold medals.

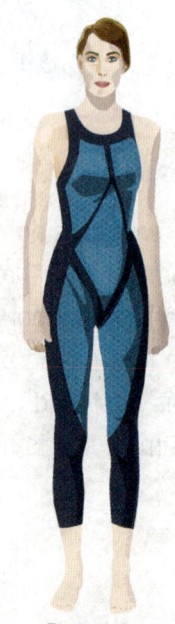

1850 - 1900

1920s

Present day

Discrimination

Recent Developments

Recent developments have encouraged **women's participation** in sport:
- The **1975 Sex Discrimination Act** emphasised women's rights.
- The Sports Council campaigns of **Sport for All** and **Come Alive** in the 1970s promoted equal opportunities.
- Men take more domestic responsibilities and more sporting activities are available.
- Child care has allowed more time to play sport.
- Establishing the **Women's Sport Foundation** in 1984 brought more women into sports administration and coaching.
- Clothing is more suited to women and the sports they participate in.
- It's considered **fashionable** and **acceptable** for women to play at **all levels**.

Women Today

Women now have a **larger role in sport**. Role models for women include:
- Cheryl Robson, mother of two and Commonwealth kickboxing champion.
- Jane Crouch, world boxing champion since 1996.
- Wendy Toms, the first woman to officiate at a Premier League football match in 1997.
- Dame Kelly Holmes, Olympic double gold medallist.

Despite changes in attitudes…
- women's sport is still regarded as **low profile** and gets a poorer media coverage, gets **less sponsorship** and smaller prize monies
- there are **fewer opportunities** for professional women's sports
- fewer women and girls take part in sport than men.

Quick Test
1. Why couldn't lower-class women play sport in the 1800s?
2. What sports were considered acceptable for upper-class women in the 1800s?
3. Who organised sport in the 1800s?
4. When was the Sex Discrimination Act passed?

KEY WORDS
Make sure you understand these words before moving on!
- Class distinction
- Sports Council campaign
- Child care
- Media coverage

Discrimination

Sport and Disability

The aim today is to focus on what disabled sportspeople **can** do rather than what they **can't** do. This has been brought about by a number of initiatives:
- The United Nations nominated 1981 as the **International Year for the Disabled** – sports councils supported this project through **Disability Sport England (1994)**.
- The **Equal Opportunities Act** made it illegal to discriminate on the grounds of disability.

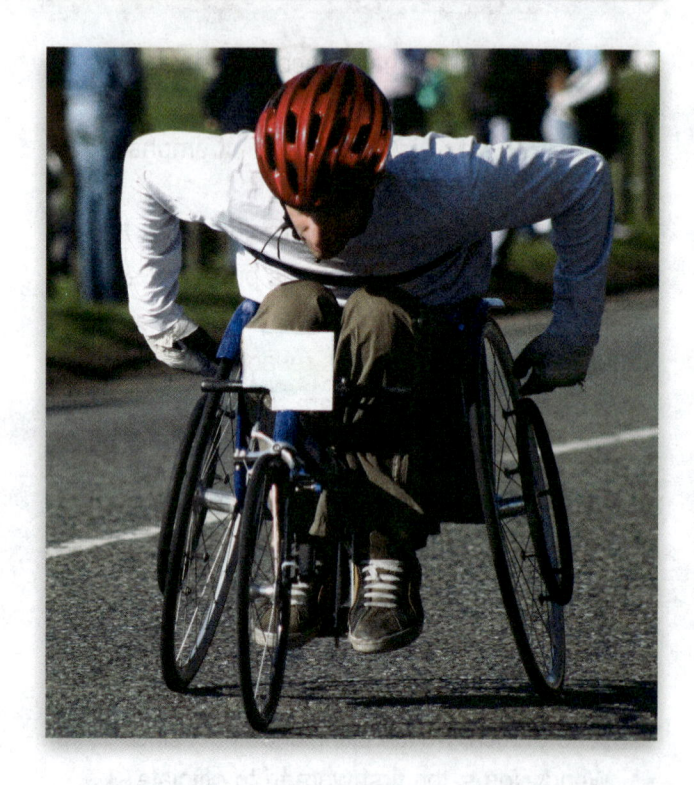

Improvements In Disabled Sports

Increased participation in **disabled sport** has developed through…
- improved facilities and **access** to sporting venues
- including disability sports in all planning
- the provision of competitions
- the involvement of the able-bodied with the disabled
- the development of **suitable equipment**, such as **lighter wheelchairs** and racing chariots
- sporting bodies **adapting their rules**, e.g. in tennis, the ball is allowed to bounce **twice**.

These moves are supported by…
- **greater media coverage**
- the inclusion of events in the Olympic Games
- the establishment of the **Paralympic Games**, which must follow all Olympic competitions.

Within Britain, all sports facilities must have…
- wider parking bays
- **ramp access** for wheelchairs
- automatic doors
- appropriate changing and toilet areas
- lifts and wider corridors.

Religion

Religion has had a significant impact on sport. In the late 19th century, Sunday was considered the 'Lord's Day' and most sport was **banned**. Playing professional sport on Sundays was banned until 1988 – most sports now occur on Sundays.

Some religions still don't allow sport on certain days. Devout Christians refuse to play on Sundays and Jewish rules don't allow play on Saturday, their Sabbath.

Some women are restricted from playing some sports owing to their **dress code**, e.g. that of the Muslim faith.

Discrimination

Ethnicity

Sports within the four home countries in Britain retain a **local identity**. This encourages pockets of popularity:
- **Cricket** tends to be seen as an **English** game.
- **Rugby** is popular in **Wales**, often at the expense of soccer.
- **Scotland** is the home of **curling**, with medals having been won at the Olympics.

Eligibility to play for a home country depends on your place of birth, or your parents' or even grandparents' place of birth. The individual has the choice.

Professional sport has developed certain restrictions:
- A county cricket team can only play a **limited number** of **overseas players**.
- Soccer had similar rules but the **Bosman ruling** in 1995 allowed professional soccer players to work in any EU country.

Changes are taking place all the time. Although the number of non-white players at all levels is increasing, they're often **made to feel unwelcome**. Some visiting international teams find they have support from British-born ethnic minority groups.

Quick Test

1. What is the focus for disabled players in sport today?
2. In what year was the International Year for the Disabled?
3. What have sporting bodies done to their rules for disabled participants?
4. What restricts many Muslim women from playing some sports?
5. Where is the home of curling?

KEY WORDS

Make sure you understand these words before moving on!
- Equal Opportunities Act
- Access
- Rule adaptation
- Paralympic Games
- Bosman ruling

Practice Questions

1 When is an individual most likely to gain sponsorship deals?

_____

2 Why can minority sports have difficulty getting sponsorship deals?

_____

_____

3 Which products would give the wrong impression to a sports sponsorship deal? Tick the correct options.

    A Alcohol ☐   **B** Hayfever medicine ☐

    C Tobacco ☐   **D** Energy drinks ☐

4 What effect can the media have on a sports schedule?

_____

_____

5 Politics can influence sport. What effect did it have on the Olympic Games in…

    a) 1964? _____

    b) 1984? _____

6 Which country was banned from sport by the Gleneagles Agreement? Tick the correct option.

    A Germany ☐   **B** USSR ☐

    C USA ☐   **D** South Africa ☐

    E France ☐   **F** Japan ☐

7 What is gamesmanship?

_____

8 Give three examples of adverse spectator behaviour.

    a) _____

    b) _____

    c) _____

Practice Questions

9 Fill in the missing words to complete the following sentences.

The .... Report made five main recommendations: the removal of perimeter ...., the .... of fans, CCTV, ... stadiums, and shared intelligence.

10 What is a semi-professional sportsman?

....

11 Who can participate in an open competition? Tick the correct option.

- A Amateurs ☐
- B Semi-professionals ☐
- C Professionals ☐
- D Anybody ☐

12 What was provided in the USA to enable amateur sports players to train in a professional manner?

....

13 What is boot money?

....

14 In what year was professional football established? Tick the correct option.

- A 1884 ☐
- B 1885 ☐
- C 1886 ☐
- D 1887 ☐

15 What did the Sports Council campaign 'Sport for All' promote?

....

16 Give three ways in which sports facilities have improved access for people with disabilities.

a) ....

b) ....

c) ....

17 Is the following statement **true** or **false**?

A player could be eligible to represent one of the home countries based on their grandparents' place of birth. ....

79

Sport in School

Promotion of Sport

Schools encourage participation in sport through…
- **compulsory lessons**:
  - National Curriculum.
  - Games for both individuals and teams.
  - Gymnastics, athletics, dance, swimming.
- **extra-curricular activities**:
  - Representative sports.
  - Sports activity clubs.
  - Residential experiences and leisure centres.
  - Links with local clubs.
  - Specialist coaching clinics.
- **awards**:
  - Sports achievement awards.
  - Sports leaders courses.
  - GCSE and A-Level exams.
  - BTEC and GNVQ vocational awards.

School Sports Activities

Activities available for schoolchildren depend on a number of conditions:
- **Facilities** in and outside school.
- The school's specialisation.
- Access to **specialist coaching**.
- **Attitudes** of teaching staff.

Schools **promote health in the curriculum** through…
- PSE
- Science
- Food Technology
- Drama
- ICT
- Health Education.

PESSCL

Physical Education, School Sport and Club Links (PESSCL) is a government initiative to encourage young people to participate in sports.

It fosters school–club links by encouraging 5 to 16-year-olds to spend at least two hours per week on PE beyond the curriculum. This will increase the number of young people playing sport outside school.

A **School Sports Coordinator** will guide children to NGB (National Governing Body) affiliated and accredited clubs.

Facilities

Providers of Facilities

There are two main categories of **facility provision**.

Local Providers:	National Providers:
• Local authorities, voluntary clubs, community partnerships, regional sports councils – run by **committees** that often employ sport development officers; **non-profit making**. • Private enterprise – commercial leisure and fitness industry, including private clubs and gyms; looks after its members but still **makes a profit**. • Private enterprise operating authority-owned facilities – local authorities privatise their facilities to the private sector, which runs it for the community but **makes a profit**.	• Sport England and Sport Governing Bodies – provide **centres of excellence** for elite athletes and developing talent. • **Voluntary organisations** such as the National Trust and Countryside Agency – provide leisure pursuit opportunities for the general public. • Private enterprise such as hotels and the AMF Ten Pin bowling centres – for **private members** and **public use**; **profit making**.

Location of Facilities

Many factors affect the location and development of a facility. These are referred to as the **6 Ps of Influence**:

- **P**ublic accessibility
- **A**ppropriate surroundings
- **P**opulation
- **P**rice
- **P**lanning permission
- **P**ublic needs

Quick Test

1. Who provides vocational awards in sport?
2. Who initiated PESSCL?
3. What does private enterprise want from sports provision?
4. Can private enterprise run a local authority facility?
5. What do the 6 Ps influence?

KEY WORDS
Make sure you understand these words before moving on!
- National Curriculum
- Extra-curricular activity
- Awards
- Specialisation
- School-Club link
- Local provider
- National provider

Organisation of Sport

Local Organisation of Sport

All sport is played by individuals but it can be very useful to belong to a club. **Local sports clubs**…
- are run **by** the members **for** the members
- **organise** facilities, fixtures and competitions
- administer the club's **paperwork**
- control **membership**.

Local sports clubs offer…
- **competitive events**
- **recreational** and social events
- coaching situations
- sports development.

Most of all, local sports clubs are the **first stepping stone to international competition**.

Organisational Structure of Competitive Sport

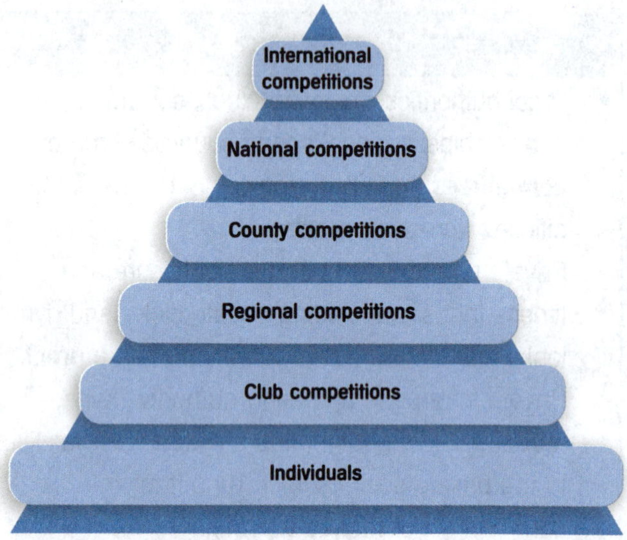

(pyramid, top to bottom)
- International competitions
- National competitions
- County competitions
- Regional competitions
- Club competitions
- Individuals

Local Club Structure

Most local clubs have a similar structure:
- **Chairman / President** – leads the club.
- **Treasurer** – deals with finance.
- **Secretary** – deals with fixtures and correspondence.
- **Club captain** – leads the players.
- **Members** – the most important people.

Many clubs also have a number of **committee members** who fulfil a range of roles, such as…
- coaching and selection
- ground and clubhouse maintenance
- fundraising
- social organisation.

National Organisation of Sport

Each sport has its own governing body. The aims of each **NGB** (**National Governing Body**) are to…
- organise and control local and national competitions
- **select teams** for international events
- **draft the rules** of the game
- establish a **coaching and refereeing structure**
- develop excellence
- foster links with the media
- **raise monies** through sponsorship, subscriptions and sales
- **provide information** to players and others
- advance the interests of the sport.

Organisation of Sport

Central Council for Physical Recreation

To promote their own interests at a **national level**, NGBs helped to establish the **Central Council for Physical Recreation** (CCPR). The main aims of the CCPR are to…

- promote the development of sport and physical recreation
- support specialist sports bodies
- develop award schemes
- act as a **consultative body** to the Sports Councils, government and others concerned with sport
- be the *collective voice* of sport: one voice speaking for many
- promote campaigns for 'Fair Play in Sport' and against 'Drugs in Sport'.

The Central Council for Physical Recreation (CCPR) also established the **British Sports Trust**, which runs the **Community Sports Leader Award Schemes** (CSLA) for local sport leaders.

CCPR members belong to **sub-divisions**:
- Games and sports
- Major spectator sports
- Movement and dance
- Outdoor pursuits
- Water recreation
- Other interested organisations.

Quick Test

1. Who are local sports clubs run for?
2. What are local clubs the first step to?
3. What is an NGB?
4. What does CCPR stand for?
5. What does the CCPR develop?

KEY WORDS
Make sure you understand these words before moving on!
- Membership
- Competitive events
- Recreational events
- National Governing Body
- Collective voice

Promoting Excellence

Raising Standards

The **structure of sport** must assist in the development of **elite performances**. There are few elite performers, but many participants. The climb to the top requires the support of an established **national coaching process**.

Sports Pyramid
- Excellence
- Performance
- Participation
- Foundation

The establishment of **Sports Coach UK** produced a **UK Coaching Framework** aimed to help athletes get to the top of their chosen sport.

UK Coaching Framework
- Individual personal coach or trainer
- National top level coaches
- Advanced coaches
- Teachers and club coaches
- Family and friends

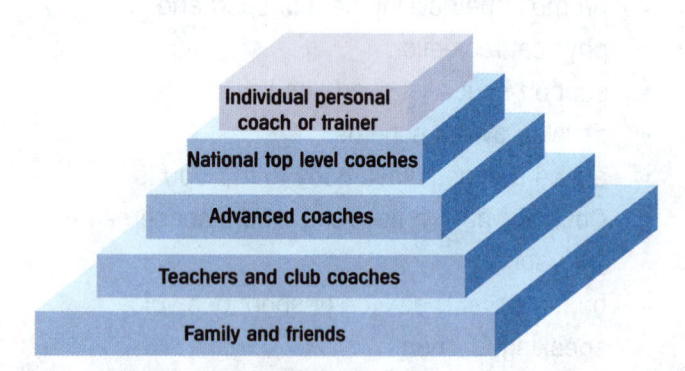

Sports Councils

Five sports councils deal with the development of UK sport: **Sport England**, **Sport Wales**, **Sport Scotland** and **Sport N Ireland** support the umbrella **UK Sport**.

The **key roles** of UK Sport are to…
- support **elite performers**
- oversee doping control, ethics and sports science
- **promote international status** by attracting major events e.g. World Cups
- coordinate all organisations within the national framework.

The **key roles** of Home Country Councils are to…
- increase **participation**
- improve the number and quality of facilities
- **raise standards** and develop excellence
- allocate lottery funding.

The sports councils are supported by the NGBs through the CCPR, via its many sub-divisions.

Basic Framework of Sport in the UK

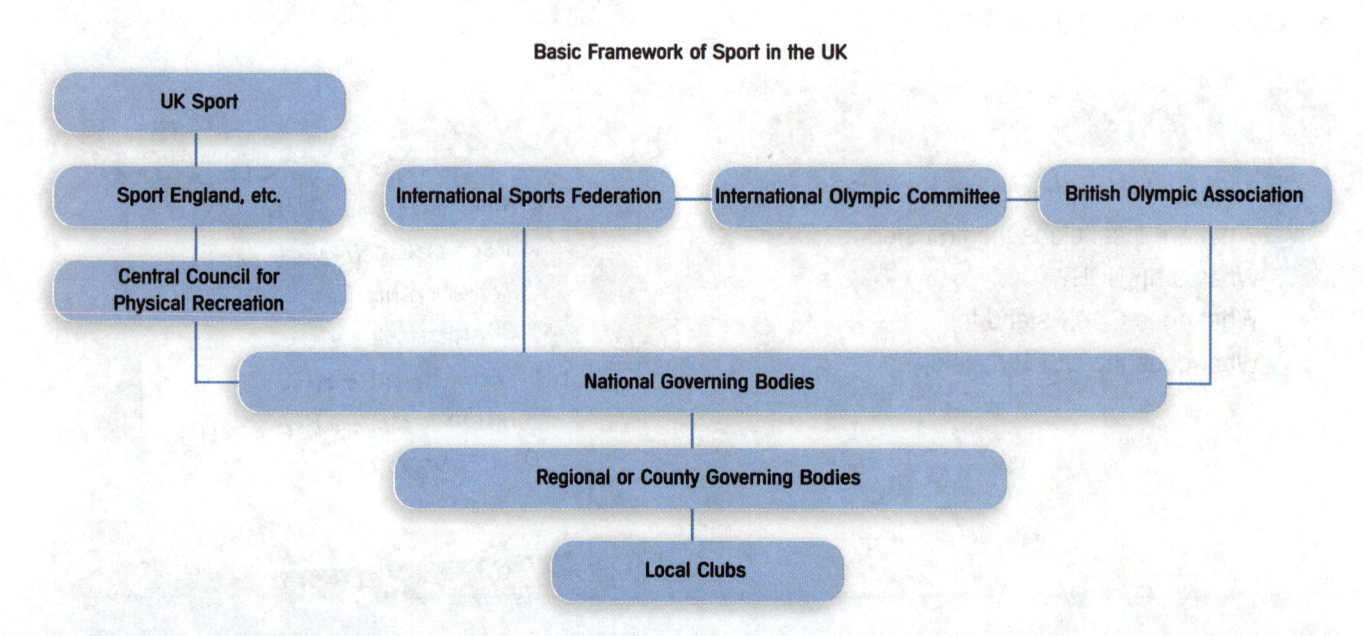

- UK Sport
- Sport England, etc.
- Central Council for Physical Recreation
- International Sports Federation
- International Olympic Committee
- British Olympic Association
- National Governing Bodies
- Regional or County Governing Bodies
- Local Clubs

Promoting Excellence

Sport England

Sport England is a **QUANGO** (**Quasi-Autonomous Non-Governmental Organisation**), set up and financed (but not controlled by) central government.

Sport England has produced a **radical new sports strategy**, aiming to meet five targets by 2012:

1. Get one million more people playing sport.
2. Reduce 16-year-olds' drop-out rate by 25%.
3. Improve talent development in at least 25 selected sports.
4. Increase people's satisfaction in playing.
5. Contribute to the delivery of the 'five hour sports offer' for young people.

National Sports Centres

National sports centres help to develop elite talent with top training, residential facilities and recreational opportunities, often hosting local, national and international events. They include…

- **Bisham Abbey** in Buckinghamshire
- **Lilleshall** in Shropshire
- **Holme Pierrepont** in Nottinghamshire
- **Plas y Brenan** in North Wales
- **EIS Sheffield** in Yorkshire.

These are complemented by the **National Velodrome** in Manchester and the **Crystal Palace** centre in London.

SPORT ENGLAND

Nine Sport England Regions: Northern, Yorkshire and Humberside, North West, Midlands, West Midlands, Eastern, South Western, Southern, London and South East.

National sports centres: Manchester, Sheffield, Lilleshall, Holme Pierrepont, Bisham Abbey, Crystal Palace.

Quick Test

1. What is on the bottom layer of a sports pyramid?
2. Who produced the UK Coaching Framework?
3. Who organises the CSLA?
4. Why is Sport England described as a QUANGO?
5. Where is the National Velodrome?

Key Words

Make sure you understand these words before moving on!

- National coaching process
- Excellence
- Performance
- Participation
- Foundation
- Elite performer
- QUANGO
- New sports strategy
- National Sports Centre

Promoting International Sport

Olympic Associations

Three major organisations concern themselves with international sport:

- The **British Olympic Association** (**BOA**) represents the country at the Olympics and is responsible for British participation. Its most notable achievement was the successful London 2012 bid.
- The **International Olympic Committee** (**IOC**) is the supreme power responsible for events connected with the Olympic Games. Its membership is drawn from representatives of all national **Olympic Associations** and the **International Sports Federation** (**ISF**).
- The International Sports Federation includes representatives from the NGB of sport from all countries and is the ultimate authority for that sport.

The **British Paralympic Association** (**BPA**) is responsible for selecting and managing Britain's team at the Paralympics. These Games take place every four years in the same city and year as the summer and winter Olympic Games.

The BPA is supported by **Disability Sport England** (**DSA**) and the **English Federation of Disability Sport** (EFDS).

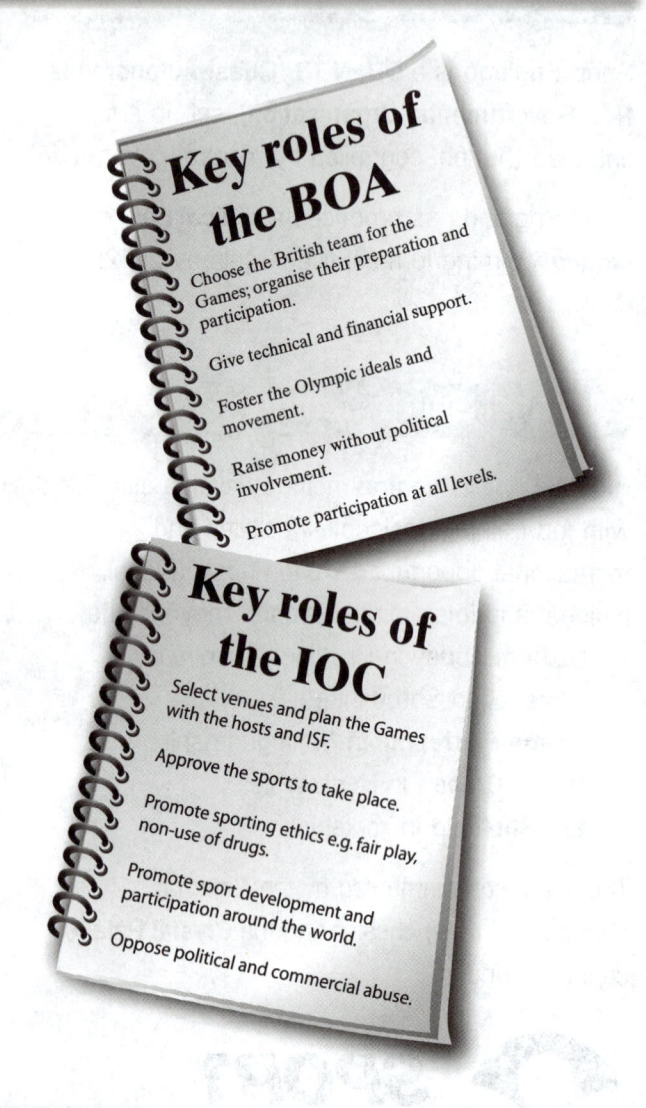

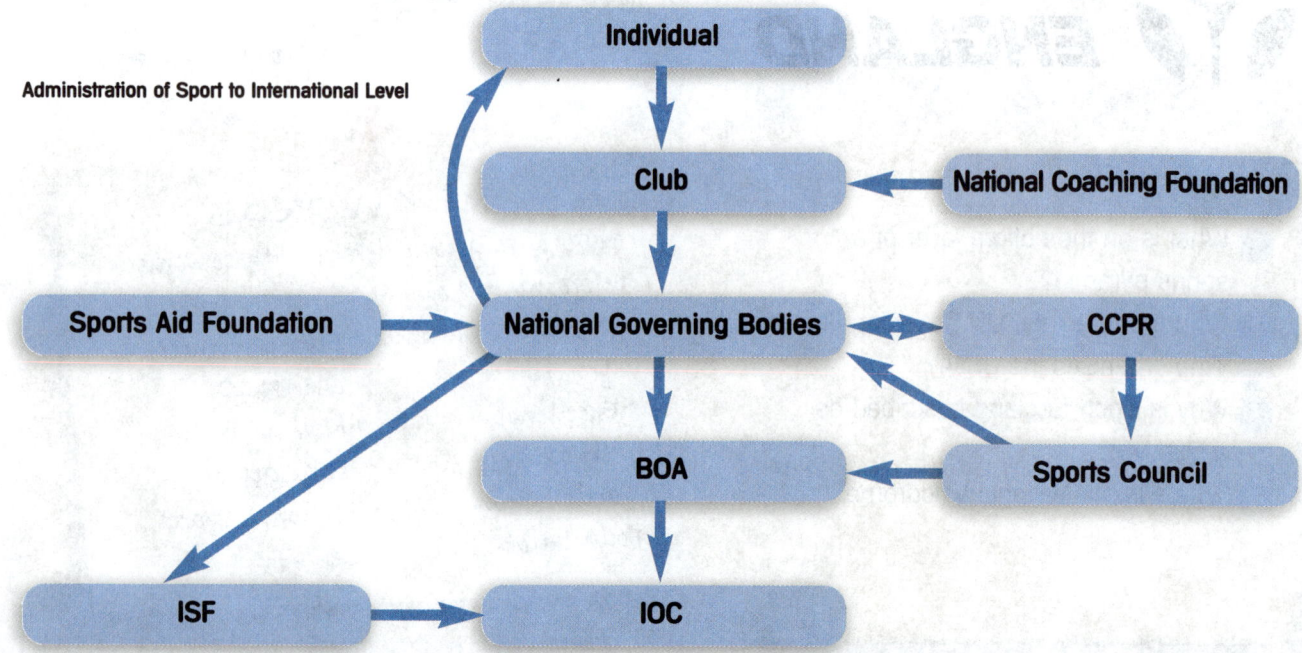

Key roles of the BOA

- Choose the British team for the Games; organise their preparation and participation.
- Give technical and financial support.
- Foster the Olympic ideals and movement.
- Raise money without political involvement.
- Promote participation at all levels.

Key roles of the IOC

- Select venues and plan the Games with the hosts and ISF.
- Approve the sports to take place.
- Promote sporting ethics e.g. fair play, non-use of drugs.
- Promote sport development and participation around the world.
- Oppose political and commercial abuse.

Administration of Sport to International Level

Funding for Sport

Main Sources of Income

Amateur sport requires **large amounts of money** to exist. Income sources include the following:

- **National Lottery**, e.g. bids can be made for grants.
- UK Sport distributes money.
- Government **taxes**, e.g. on gambling.
- Broadcasting rights and sponsorship.
- NGBs.
- Private investment.
- Membership fees.
- **Earned income**, entrance monies, raffles and hospitality income.

Professional clubs often **need more money** than amateur clubs but tend to have a **bigger outlay**.

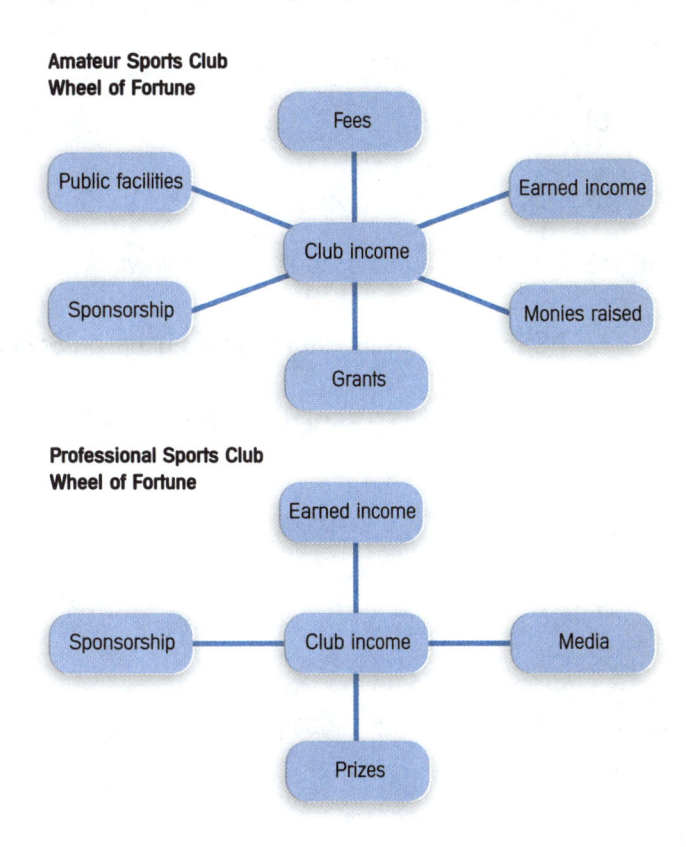

Amateur Sports Club Wheel of Fortune

Club income: Fees, Earned income, Monies raised, Grants, Sponsorship, Public facilities

Professional Sports Club Wheel of Fortune

Club income: Earned income, Media, Prizes, Sponsorship

National Lottery

Sport is a **good cause** that receives income from the National Lottery (**Lotto**), established in 1994.

For every £1 spent on a lottery ticket, 28 pence goes to good causes. Originally, just under 6 pence went to sport but more is expected to be spent on the 2012 Games.

The lottery is a **primary source of funding** for these Games, based not only in London but in other parts of the country.

Sport England directs lottery funds to sports through their NGBs for both capital and recurrent costs.

Quick Test

1. What does the BOA choose?
2. What does the IOC select?
3. Who is the supreme power at an Olympic Games?
4. Who directs lottery funds to sport in England?
5. What does the BPA choose?

KEY WORDS
Make sure you understand these words before moving on!
- BOA
- IOC
- ISF
- BPA
- DSA
- Earned income
- Lotto

Practice Questions

1 Give three ways in which schools encourage participation in sport.

a) ....

b) ....

c) ....

2 a) Circle the correct options in the following sentence.

PESSCL stands for the Physical Education **School** / **State** Sports **Class** / **Club** Links.

b) How does the PESSCL foster these links?

....

....

3 Many factors affect the location and development of a facility. Name three of the 6 Ps of Influence.

a) ....

b) ....

c) ....

4 Who organises and controls local and national competitions in a sport? Tick the correct option.

A National Granting Body ☐

B National Governing Body ☐

C International Granting Body ☐

D International Governing Body ☐

5 Match **A**, **B**, **C** and **D** with the labels **1–4** on the sports pyramid.

A Performance ☐

B Foundation ☐

C Excellence ☐

D Participation ☐

Practice Questions

6 a) Name the five sports councils.

i) .... ii) .... iii) ....

iv) .... v) ....

b) Which of these is the umbrella sports council?

....

7 Choose the correct words from the options given to complete the sentence below.

| participation | facilities | lottery | strategies |
| funding | centres | bank | crowds |

The four major roles of the home country sports councils are to increase ...., improve ...., raise standards and allocate .... funding.

8 Name the four National Sports Centres in England.

a) ....

b) ....

c) ....

d) ....

9 Who do the National Sports Centres cater for besides elite performers?

....

10 What event happens in the same place and in the same year as the Olympic Games?

....

11 What do the following terms stand for?

a) BOA ....

b) IOC ....

c) ISF ....

d) EFDS ....

Appendix

Tables of Norms

Reminder – these tables are an indication only of levels attained. Incorrect test protocol can affect their validity.

A1 Rating Table for Suppleness

Rating	Shoulder Lift	Sit and Reach
Very Good	36+	10+
Good	25+	5+
Fair	20+	0+
Poor	15+	-5

All scores are in cm

A2 Rating Table for Strength

Rating	Standing Long Jump	Standing High Jump	Sit-ups
Very Good	190+	65+	25+
Good	170+	60+	20+
Fair	150+	50+	16+
Poor	130+	40+	14+

Scores for Standing Long Jump and Standing High jump in cm

A3 Rating for Cardiovascular Endurance

Rating	Step Test	12-Minute Run	
		Male	Female
Very Good	90+	2600+	2200+
Good	80+	2400+	2000+
Fair	65+	2200+	1800+
Poor	50+	2000+	1700+

Scores for 12-minute run in metres

A4 Rating Table for Agility

Time in Seconds		Rating
Male	Female	
Less than 15.2	Less than 17.0	Excellent
16.1–15.2	17.9–17.0	Good
18.1–16.2	21.7–18.0	Average
19.3–18.2	23.0–21.8	Fair
More than 19.3	More than 23.0	Poor

Glossary

Active stretching – the moving of the joint beyond the point of resistance by the performer.
Adverse spectator behaviour – hooliganism.
Aerobic – activity that takes place with oxygen.
Aerobic exercise – activity of low intensity and long duration, with a plentiful supply of oxygen.
Aerobic threshold – minimum level of intensity of training for it to be effective.
Agility – combination of flexibility and speed, the ability to change body position quickly and accurately.
Agonist – prime mover muscle that contributes to a movement at a joint.
Amino acids – proteins in digested form in the bloodstream.
Anabolic steroid – performance-enhancing drug that can increase muscle mass, strength and power.
Anaerobic exercise – activity of high intensity and short duration, performed without oxygen.
Anaerobic threshold – level of intensity of training above which the individual needs more than oxygen to meet energy demands.
Antagonist – muscle that opposes the action of, and helps regulate, the agonist.
Arousal – the body's state of preparedness for action.
Balance – the ability to retain a stable position in relation to either the static or dynamic environment.
Ballistic stretching – using the momentum of the body to stretch a joint.
Beta-blocker – performance-enhancing drug that has a calming and relaxing effect.
Blood doping – blood transfusion to a competitor in the belief that it will increase the oxygen-carrying capacity; a banned procedure. See EPO.
Body composition – the percentage of body weight that is muscle, bone and fat.
Bradycardia – a decreased or slow resting heart rate associated with endurance training.
Carbo-loading – the increase of carbohydrates in the diet in the belief it will produce an increase of energy levels for endurance activities.
Cardiac output – the amount of blood pumped from the heart in one minute.
Cardiovascular endurance (aerobic fitness) – the ability of the heart and lungs to supply oxygen via the bloodstream to provide energy to carry on with physical activity.
Cardiovascular fitness – the ability of the circulatory and respiratory systems to work effectively for long periods of time.
Cardiovascular system – the circulation of blood and the transportation of oxygen and waste products to and from the cells of the body.
Cartilage (articular) – tough tissue that covers the ends of bones and provides a smooth surface for movement.
Cartilage (menisci) – the semi-lunar discs of fibro cartilage separating the ends of bones in some joints; act as shock absorbers.
Circulatory system – the heart, blood and blood vessels.
Closed skills – an action that is internally paced, regardless of the environment.
Complex skill – a skill that includes a number of basic skills.
Concentric contraction – a form of isometric contraction when the muscle fibres shorten.
Coordination – the ability to link the use of two or more body parts.
CO_2 – carbon dioxide, a waste product within the body.
Dehydration – the loss of water to the body.
Diuretic – performance-enhancing drug that increases urination, often used for rapid weight loss or as a masking agent for other substances.
Dynamic strength – the ability to maintain muscular force over a prolonged period of time.
Eccentric contraction – when the muscle fibres lengthen under tension.
Ectomorph – body type that features narrow shoulders and hips, and thinness.
Endomorph – body type that features wide hips, narrow shoulders and a large fat content.
EPO (erythropoietin) – artificial peptide hormone that mimics the actions of blood doping; a banned substance.
Exercise – healthy physical activity.

Glossary

Explosive strength – the ability to exert muscular force in a series of strong, sudden movements.
Extrinsic feedback – information received from outside the performer.
Fitness – the ability to meet the demands of the environment.
FITT – Frequency, Intensity, Time, Type: the principles of training.
Fixed load – when an exercise is performed continually for a given time in a circuit.
Flexibility – total range of movement at a joint.
Individual load – when an exercise is performed at a level fixed by the performer in a circuit.
Intrinsic feedback – information received from within the performer.
Isometric contractions – when muscles contract but the fibres stay the same length and no movement takes place.
Isotonic contractions – when muscles contract, the fibres shorten and movement takes place.
KP – Knowledge of Performance.
KR – Knowledge of Results.
Lactic acid – poisonous by-product of exercise.
Mesomorph – body type that features wide shoulders, narrow hips and strong muscularity.
Motivation – the determination to win.
Muscular endurance – the ability to use skeletal muscles for a long time.
Muscular strength – the amount of force that a muscle can exert against a resistance.
Narcotic analgesic – performance-enhancing drug that reduces the feeling of pain.
Open skills – skills used in changing situations.
Overload – working at a level higher than normal.
Oxygen debt (O_2 debt) – the amount of oxygen consumed during recovery from exhaustion.
Passive stretching – moving the joint beyond the point of resistance with the aid of a partner.
Peaking – training to be at the optimum state of readiness for a specific event.
Peptide hormone – performance-enhancing drug that causes the production of other hormones.

PESSCL – PE and School Sport Clubs Links.
Power – a combination of speed and strength.
Progressive overload – a gradual increase of overload to reflect training success.
Reaction time – time taken to respond to a stimulus.
Recovery – time taken by the body to return to the normal state.
Rest – period of time allocated for recovery.
Reversibility – the atrophy that results when training ceases.
Skill – a learned predetermined action performed with economy of effort.
SMART – Specific, Measurable, Achievable, Realistic, Time.
Somatotypes – body classification system.
Specificity – the matching of training to the requirements of the activity.
Speed – time taken to move the body or a body part a specific distance.
Stamina – maximum duration an activity can be maintained; also known as endurance or staying power.
Stimulant – performance-enhancing drug that increases the activity of the cardiovascular and nervous systems.
Stroke volume – the volume of blood pumped out by the left ventricle in one beat.
Target zone – the pulse range within which an individual needs to work for training to be effective.
Training – a programme of exercise designed to improve fitness and / or develop skill acquisition.
TTR – Training Threshold Rate.

Answers

Body Systems

Quick Test Answers

Page 5
1. 206
2. In the long bones
3. Vertebral column and the bones connected to it
4. Ribs
5. Vertebrae

Page 9
1. a) Shoulder
   b) Calf
   c) Bottom
2. Gut or blood vessel walls
3. Agonist
4. Fast twitch
5. They stay the same length

Page 11
1. Between the ribs
2. Breathe out
3. Lungs
4. The number of breaths per minute
5. Low intensity

Page 13
1. Atria
2. The body
3. Pulmonary veins
4. Aorta

Page 15
1. Water
2. It goes up
3. In white blood cells
4. Cardiac output increases
5. Pulse rate increases

Answers to Practice Questions

Page 16
1. a) Patella
   b) Sternum
   c) Tibia
   d) Femur
2. a)–d) **In any order:** Protection; Blood production; Movement; Support
3. a)–e) **In any order:** Cervical; Thoracic; Lumbar; Sacral; Coccyx
4. a) Cartilage
   b) Tendon
5. a) The joint closes
   b) The joint moves away
6. Alveoli
7. The diaphragm moves up and the ribs move down.

Page 17
8. a)–c) **In any order:** Skeletal – Attached to bones; Smooth – Gut; Cardiac – Heart
9. a) i)–iv) **In any order:** Plasma; Platelets; Red cells, White cells
   b) i) Red cells
      ii) White cells
10. [Heart/circulation diagram labelled: Lungs; right atria; left atria; right ventricle; left ventricle; Body]

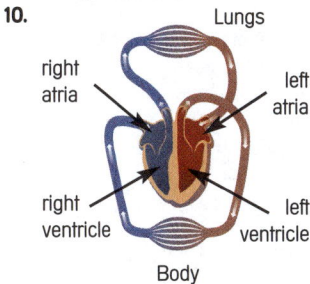

Fitness & Training

Quick Test Answers

Page 19
1. Health and fitness
2. It doubles
3. It trebles
4. Body composition
5. False

Page 21
1. Agility
2. Stamina
3. Glucose
4. Power

Page 23
1. Frequency
   Intensity
   Time
   Type
2. Increase frequency; Increase intensity; Increase time; Changing the type of exercise to suit workload
3. One week
4. Measurable
5. Intrinsic and extrinsic

Page 25
1. Training Threshold Rate
2. Aerobic
3. Under supervision
4. Prolonged
5. Rest periods

Page 29
1. Work and rest
2. Long slow distance
3. Speed play
4. Body momentum
5. Sets
6. The weights

Page 34
1. Warm-up
2. Warm-up; Fitness; Skill; Cool down
3. It gets faster
4. The muscles get bigger
5. 37°C

Answers to Practice Questions

Page 38
1. a)–c) **In any order:** Social; Mental; Physical
2. a)–e) **In any order:** Strength; Speed; Suppleness; Stamina; Somatotype
3. a) Maximum force against immovable object
   b) Maximum force in one movement
   c) Repeated application of same force
4. a) somatotype
   b) oxygen
   c) glucose
5. S = Specific
   M = Measurable
   A = Agreed and achievable
   R = Realistic and recorded
   T = Time-phased
6. lactic

Page 39
7. increase
8. A
9. True
10. **In any order:** Work; Rest
11. Fartlek training
12. a) best; specific
    b) bigger; resting; red
13. a)–c) **Any three from:** Prepare body for work; Prepare mind for work; Raise heart rate; Raise breathing levels; Reduce possibility of injury
14. a) Grip dynamometer
    b) Sit and reach
    c) Illinois run
    d) Stork Stand

93

Answers

Factors Affecting Performance

Quick Test Answers
Page 41
1. Body shape
2. Very thin
3. Makes you bigger and stronger
4. Respiratory system
5. No

Page 43
1. Minerals; Protein; Water; Fat; Vitamins; Carbohydrates; Fibre
2. Endurance performers
3. Protein
4. Positive attitude
5. Physical wellbeing

Page 45
1. Learned
2. Predetermined
3. Early age
4. Inside the body
5. Outside the body

Page 47
1. Steroids
2. Relax the body
3. Painkillers
4. Stimulants
5. Blood doping

Answers to Practice Questions
Page 48
1. Performance levels are high when young, but they decrease with age.
2. A; D
3. For future childbirth.
4. a) thinner; lower
   b) Carbohydrates; Protein; Vitamins; Fats; Fibre; Water; Minerals.
5. extra; stamina
6. A; B
7. a)–b) Any two suitable examples, e.g. Hayfever medicine; Asthma treatment; Prescribed drugs

Page 49
8. pain
9. C
10. a)–c) **In any order:** Physical, Social, Mental
11. a)–c) **In any order:** Work / School; Physical exercise; Relaxation
12. D
13. a) Open
    b) Variable
14. a)–c) **In any order:** Visual; Verbal; Manual
15. a) KP = Knowledge of performance
    b) KR = Knowledge of results

Participation in Sport

Quick Test Answers
Page 51
1. Leisure time
2. They run campaigns
3. Some environments are better for doing activities
4. A sense of achievement
5. Peers

Page 53
1. Peer groups
2. Specific age groups
3. Verrucas
4. Gum shields
5. Cure

Page 55
1. Individual
2. Seeded
3. All other teams
4. National organisations
5. Sports etiquette

Page 57
1. Man-made
2. Foam mats
3. Skill performance
4. They help to identify an athlete's strengths and weaknesses
5. Sensors record the position of runners

Page 59
1. Dust or water
2. Magnesium carbonate
3. Protective equipment
4. Body suits
5. Neoprene

Page 61
1. Walk
2. When planning an outdoor trip
3. Vertically
4. Straight
5. Injury

Answers to Practice Questions
Page 62
1. Spare time
2. A
3. Your friends / classmates
4. As you get older you participate less in fewer activities.
5. bacteria; washing
6. Ladders, Leagues, Knockout
7. The best players / teams are identified early on so they can be arranged to meet near the final.
8. a) referee / umpire
   b sportsmanship

Page 63
9. C
10. Heart rate monitors
11. reduce
12. **Any three suitable answers,** e.g. Swimmers, cyclists, skaters, athletes.
13. False
14. a) Risk
    b) designated; aids
15. up; arms; straight; leg

94

Answers

Issues in Sport

Quick Test Answers
Page 65
1. Commercial transaction
2. Material support
3. Promotion
4. Minority sports

Page 67
1. Television
2. Finance
3. It can decline
4. Undermine them
5. FA Cup Final; Wimbledon

Page 69
1. Minister for Sport
2. National Lottery
3. Russian invasion of Hungary
4. Rhodesia
5. 1977

Page 71
1. Tensions
2. Respect and courtesy
3. Violent crowd behaviour
4. 1970s and 1980s
5. The Taylor Report

Page 73
1. Paid
2. A job
3. Anybody
4. Training expenses
5. Professionalism

Page 75
1. No time or money
2. Riding, walking, badminton, tennis
3. Men
4. 1975

Page 77
1. To show what they can do rather than what they can't do.
2. 1981
3. Adapted the rules
4. Dress code
5. Scotland

Answers to Practice Questions
Page 78
1. When they are successful in their sport.
2. They are less well known and sponsors want a bigger audience.
3. A; C
4. It can dictate a change
5. a) 1964 – S Africa forced to withdraw
   b) 1984 – USSR boycott
6. D
7. Timewasting
8. **Any three suitable answers,** e.g. Swearing, abuse, fighting.

Page 79
9. Taylor; fences; segregation; all-seater
10. Someone paid to play who also has a job.
11. D
12. Sports scholarships
13. Illegal payments to amateurs
14. A
15. Equal opportunities in sport
16. **Any three from:** Wider parking bays; Ramp access; Automatic doors; Appropriate changing facilities, Lifts; Wider corridors
17. True

Organisation and Structure

Quick Test Answers
Page 81
1. BTEC and GNVQ
2. The government
3. Profit
4. Yes
5. Location and development of a facility

Page 83
1. Members
2. International competition
3. National Governing Body
4. Central Council for Physical Recreation
5. Award schemes

Page 85
1. Foundation
2. Sports Coach UK
3. CCPR
4. It is set up and financed (but not controlled by) central government.
5. Manchester

Page 87
1. The British Olympic team
2. The venue for Olympic Games
3. IOC
4. Sport England
5. The British Paralympic team

Answers to Practice Questions
Page 88
1. a)–c) **In any order:** Through the National Curriculum; Extra-curricular activities; Awards
2. a) School, Club
   b) It encourages 5 to 16-year-olds to spend at least two hours per week on PE beyond the curriculum.
3. **Any three from:** Price; Planning permission; Public needs; Population; Public accessibility; Appropriate surroundings
4. B
5. A2; B4; C1; D3

Page 89
6. a) i)–v) **In any order:** Sport England; Sport Scotland; Sport Wales; Sport N. Ireland; Sport UK
   b) Sport UK
7. participation; facilities; lottery
8. a)–d) **In any order:** Bisham Abbey; Lilleshall; Holme Pierrepont; EIS Sheffield
9. Recreational users
10. Paralympic Games
11. a) British Olympic Association
    b) International Olympic Committee
    c) International Sports Federation
    d) English Federation of Disability Sport

Index

A
Aerobic exercise 11, 25
Aerobic fitness 20
Aerobic programmes 30
Anaerobic exercise 11, 25
Anaerobic fitness 20
Aqua aerobics 30

B
Blood pressure 14
Blood vessels 13
Body conditioning programmes 30
Bones 4
Breathing 10

C
Carrying 61
CCPR 83
Circuit training 27
Circulatory system 12–13
Clothing 58, 74
Competitions 54
Continuous training 28

D
Diet 42–43
Disability 76
Drugs 46–47

E
Effects of exercise 15, 33
Environment 40
Ethnicity 77

F
Facilities 81
Fartlek training 28
Fast twitch fibres 9
Feedback 45
Fitness tests 35–36
Flexibility training 28
Football hooliganism 71
Funding 87

G
Gaseous exchange 10–11
Gender 40

H
Health and hygiene 53
Heart 12

I
Interval training 28

J
Joints 7–8

L
Leisure 50
Lifting 61

M
Media 66–67
Mental benefits of exercise 18
Modern technology 56–57
Motivation 23

Motor fitness 21
Muscle contractions 9
Muscles 9–10

N
National sports centres 85

O
Olympic associations 86
Organisation of sport 82–83
Oxygen debt 24

P
Participation 52
Peaking 31
Periodisation 31
PESSCL 80
Physical benefits of exercise 19
Physical fitness 19, 20
Physique 40
Pilates 30
Politics 68–69
Posture 21
Principles of training 22
Pulse 12

R
Religion 76
Respiratory system 10–11

S
Safety 59–60
School sports 80
Seasonal sports 31
Shunt vessel system 33
Skeleton 4
Skill 44–45
Skill tests 37
Slow twitch fibres 9
Social benefits 18
Social benefits of exercise 18
Spectators 70–71
Sponsorship 64–65
Sport England 85
Sporting behaviour 55, 70–71
Sporting status 72–73
Sports councils 84
Sports etiquette 55
Step aerobics 30
Synovial joint 6

T
Tests for balance 37
Tests for cardiovascular fitness 36
Tests for local muscular stamina 36
Tests of reaction 37
Tests of skill 37
Tests of speed 37
Tests of strength 35
Tests of suppleness 35
Training targets 23
Training threshold rate 24
Training venues 31

V
Vertebral column 5

W
Warm-ups 32
Warm-downs 32
Weight training 26
Women in sport 74–75

Y
Yoga 30